House Plant IDENTIFIER

By HELMUT BECHTEL

With photographs by the author
and drawings by Gabriele Gossner and Sigrid Haag

STERLING PUBLISHING CO., Inc., New York

Oak Tree Press Co., Ltd. London & Sydney

OTHER BOOKS OF INTEREST

Cage Bird Identifier
Colorful Mineral Identifier
Tropical Fish Identifier

Second Printing, 1974

© 1973 by Sterling Publishing Co, Inc.
419 Park Avenue South, New York 10016
British edition published by
Oak Tree Press Co., Ltd., Nassau, Bahamas
Distributed in Australia
and New Zealand by Oak Tree Press Co., Ltd.,
P.O. Box J34, Brickfield Hill, Sydney 2000, N.S.W.
Distributed in the United Kingdom
and elsewhere in the British Commonwealth
by Ward Lock Ltd., 116 Baker Street, London W 1

Adapted from the German book "Die Bunte Welt der Zimmer-
blumen" by Helmut Bechtel. Photos by Helmut Bechtel.
© 1969 by Franck'sche Verlagshandlung, Stuttgart, West
Germany. Translated by Manly Banister. Adapted by
E. W. Egan.

Library of Congress Catalog Card No.: 72–95203
Sterling ISBN 0–8069-3056–X Trade   Oak Tree 7061–2433–2
3057–8 Library
Printed in
Hong Kong

CONTENTS

Flowers for Table and Window-Sill

Our enthusiasm is often aroused by the splendid coloration and infinite variety of form of our house plants. Often we wonder: What is this plant called? How should it be cared for? Where does it come from? This book will help you answer these questions for 120 beautiful house plants. Along with many well known and easy-to-care-for plants, you will find some especially beautiful and spectacular species that must be cared for with a somewhat more experienced and devoted hand.

PLANT NAMES

The scientific names of the primary stock are given in cases where the plants have been considerably changed and made more beautiful by horticultural selection. The sign *x* within the scientific name indicates a hybrid, that is, a form created by crossing different species. In the scientific names, the first name given indicates the GENUS, the second the SPECIES (a genus usually consists of several species). A third element in the scientific name, indicates the VARIETY (var.).

It is desirable to give house plants living conditions that most closely approximate those of their original homeland. For this purpose, we must know from what climate they come and what kind of environment they prefer.

SUNLIGHT

All green plants need light. It provides the energy required for photosynthesis, an involved chemical process by means of which plants build organic materials out of carbon dioxide (carbonic acid gas). Nevertheless, only a few house plants can withstand direct sunlight. If you place them in a strongly sunlit, south window, you must also take care that they will be shaded during the time that the sun shines most strongly. A pull-down blind is the best means of providing shade, but a paper screen will also serve. The result of exposure to too strong sunlight is yellow or brown "burned" leaves.

AIR

Plants breathe supplementary carbon dioxide gas from the air. Part of plant care therefore consists of draft-free air circulation. Draft-free— this is important, strange as it may seem, for plants can also catch cold. Especially hungry for fresh air are the so-called epiphytes. These are plants which, in the wild live on trees at airy heights (many orchids, for instance) without being parasitic to the tree.

TEMPERATURE

In modern, heated rooms, it is not difficult to provide the plants with an evenly regulated temperature. However, it is not so easy to maintain a *low* enough temperature, as needed by many plants during their resting period. Plants from the Mediterranean countries and other temperate regions must be kept much cooler during their winter resting period than is possible in a heated room. A frost-free yet quite bright cellar space is ideal for this, but not possible for apartment-dwellers. Succulents ("thick-leaved" plants) from desert and steppe regions also require lower temperatures during their resting period. This holds good especially for Cacti, Living Stones and many plants of the Spurge Family.

HUMIDITY

Many warmth-loving plants from the tropics not only need sufficient warmth, but, even more important, they must have high humidity. These plants should be sprayed daily with lukewarm, soft water—preferably rain water. But be careful—many flowers cannot stand direct spraying.

WATERING

Watering is the most important task in plant care. Too much water can do a great deal of damage to many plants. When the earth in the flower pot is continually too wet, decay sets in, and especially, the pore-filling water prevents the air from entering the soil—the roots can no longer breathe and they die.

Bromeliads or Pineapple plants (*Bromeliaceae*) in nature receive the greatest part of their moisture from rain water, which collects in the hollow at the base of each leaf. When they are grown as house plants, water them in the same way.

FERTILIZER

During their period of growth, house plants also need mineral nourishment, which can be provided for them in the form of solid or liquid fertilizer. Too much fertilizer is damaging, especially to epiphytic orchids, which require hardly any fertilizing.

POISONOUS PLANTS

A warning should be given here. A few house plants are poisonous. These must be placed in such a location that small children—known for stuffing everything they see into their mouths—cannot reach them.

How to Use This Pocket Guide

Suppose you have just received as a gift a plant that is unknown to you. What is it called? How do you care for it? Is it described and illustrated in this book?

On pages 10 and 11 is a pictorial table. Using it will help you find in the index the pages on which your plant can be found.

Look for answers to the following questions in the ranks of the table:

1. Is it a fern? (Dark spore groups on the undersides of leaves.)

2. Are the leaves shaped like needles?

3. Are leaves or stem fleshy (succulent)?

4. Is it a bulb—or tuber-type plant?

5. Does the plant have typical orchidlike flowers?

6. Do the plant's runners, leaves or sprouts tend to hang downwards?

7. Is the plant a creeper, twiner or climber?

8. Does the plant bear beautiful, multi-colored fruit?

9. If you cannot answer any of these questions with "yes," one possibility still remains. You have

a plant that is kept mainly for its vivid and beautiful blooms or its exotic foliage.

If you already know the name of the plant—the florist will gladly tell you what you are buying—a glance into the index on pages 252–256 will be sufficient to locate the proper page.

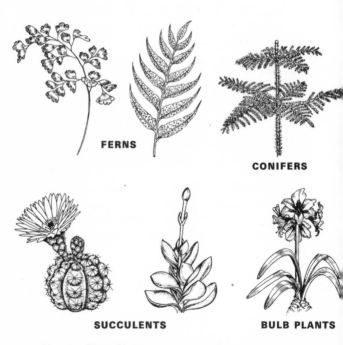

FERNS

CONIFERS

SUCCULENTS

BULB PLANTS

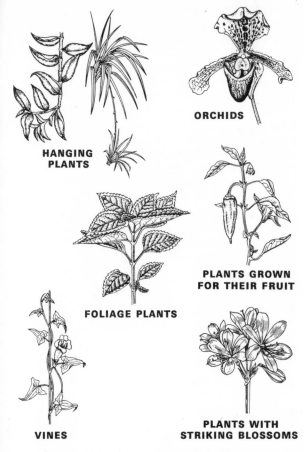

HANGING PLANTS

ORCHIDS

FOLIAGE PLANTS

PLANTS GROWN FOR THEIR FRUIT

VINES

PLANTS WITH STRIKING BLOSSOMS

POPULAR NAME: **Staghorn Fern**
SCIENTIFIC NAME: *Platycerium alcicorne*
FAMILY: *Polypodiaceae* (Polypody)

This fern hails from the forests of tropical northern Australia; other species come from Southeast Asia, Africa and South America. All are *epiphytic*, that is, they are plants that take root on trees or rocks but are not *parasitic*—parasites draw nourishment from the plants they grow on. Epiphytes have aerial roots which draw water from the air. *Platycerium alcicorne* belongs to the most resistant group of staghorn ferns.

CARE: It requires a warm location throughout the year with high humidity; however, it is considerably less sensitive to temperature fluctuations than many other species. Its root-ball must not be allowed to dry out. For this reason, dip the pot in lukewarm water once a week. Now and then, add a little fertilizer to the water.

Staghorn Fern

POPULAR NAME: **Sword Brake**
SCIENTIFIC NAME: *Pteris ensiformis*
FAMILY: *Polypodiaceae* (Polypody)

The original species of these brakes is spread over a wide region of tropical Asia, Australia and Polynesia. The cultivated forms with variegated leaves are very popular, especially the green-and-white striped ones; unfortunately, these forms are somewhat more delicate than the plain green varieties.

CARE: Brakes, like other ferns, should be given a shady location with high humidity. They should be plentifully watered in summer, preferably with rain water. Fertilize at intervals of about three weeks. For wintering over, put the brake in a cool room (8 to 10° C or 46 to 50° F). The cultivated forms of these ferns, with variegated leaves, should be kept somewhat warmer.

Sword Brake

POPULAR NAMES: **Brittle or Fan Maiden Hair Fern**
SCIENTIFIC NAME: *Adiantum tenerum*
FAMILY: *Polypodiaceae* (Polypody)

Tropical America and the West Indies are the homelands of *Adiantum tenerum*. Cultivated varieties are found on the market more often than the original type. Especially liked is the cultivated form illustrated here, "Scutum Roseum."

CARE: The Maiden Hair Fern requires high humidity. This is obtained by spraying the plant often and by placing it in a pan or dish kept constantly full of water. Support the pot in such a way that it is above the water so that the roots are not standing in it. A bright but shady location is most suitable for the Maiden Hair Fern, which can winter over at a warmer temperature than the Sword Brake.

Maiden Hair Fern

POPULAR NAME: **Norfolk Island Pine**
SCIENTIFIC NAME: *Araucaria excelsa*
FAMILY: *Araucariaceae (Araucaria)*

In its native haunt, Norfolk Island, between Australia and New Zealand, this tree can grow to 65 metres (213 feet) high. In the Mediterranean region the Araucaria when planted outdoors can reach a stately height of 20 metres (65 feet).

CARE: The Araucaria, a dwarf tree when cultivated as a house plant, thrives only in cool, bright rooms. It must be protected from bright sun. During the summer, the Norfolk Island Pine is best kept out of doors, or in a room that is really well ventilated. It should not be watered too much, but sprayed often. In its winter resting period, it requires a temperature ranging from 3 to 10° C or 38 to 50° F. Watering should then be stopped almost completely. In winter the Norfolk Island Pine should be kept in a well lighted place.

Norfolk Island Pine

POPULAR NAME: **Rubber Plant**
SCIENTIFIC NAME: *Ficus elastica*
FAMILY: *Moraceae* (Mulberry)

Southeast Asia and the Malay Archipelago are the homelands of this popular plant, and in those regions it grows to a height of from 20 to 25 metres (65 to 82 feet). Most often seen as a house plant is the original green-leaved variety, though the cultivated variety illustrated here with green and cream leaves, "Variegata," is a desirable house plant.

CARE: A half-shaded, warm place is the proper location for the Rubber Plant. During the summer, it requires a great deal of water. During this time of year it can also be kept in the open. In the winter, temperatures between 15 to 18° C or 59 to 64° F suit it best. The form with variegated leaves is somewhat more sensitive and warmth-loving than the plain green variety.

Rubber Plant

POPULAR NAMES: **Bougainvillea, Paper Flower**
SCIENTIFIC NAME: *Bougainvillea glabra*
FAMILY: *Nyctaginaceae* (Four-O'Clock)

Brazil is the native land of this luxuriantly blooming, climbing bush, which is now found throughout
the tropics. It may climb to a height of 3 to 4
metres (10 to 12 feet). When it is grown as a house
plant, the blooms appear as a rule in summer. The
flowers themselves are small and are a plain,
yellowish white. The real attraction is the red or
bright violet involucres (whorl of small bracts or
modified leaves supporting the flower), which
outlast the blossoms.

CARE: In summer, the Bougainvillea is kept in a
warm, sunny place; it can be put out of doors in a
sheltered spot. During this time the plant requires
considerable water and fertilizer. In its resting
period—which is likely to last from four to six
weeks—it must stay cool (5 to 10° C or 41 to 50° F)
and dry.

Bougainvillea

POPULAR NAMES: **Crab Cactus, Christmas Cactus**
SCIENTIFIC NAME: *Zygocactus truncatus*
FAMILY: *Cactaceae* (Cactus)

This wild variety of the Christmas Cactus comes from Brazil's Organ Mountains and is the ancestor of many white, carmine and pink cultivated varieties now available such as the one illustrated, called "Christmas Joy." It blooms in northern climates in December and January, and is similar to the more familiar, true Christmas Cactus, *Schlumbergera bridgesii*.

CARE: Unlike most familiar cacti, the Christmas Cactus lives epiphytically in subtropical forests and for this reason needs more moisture and less sun than cacti from arid regions—however, overwetting will damage the plant. In summer, keep the Christmas Cactus rather warm, and in a spot in open shade; in the winter, keep it in a spot that is bright and not too cool (about 15° C or 59° F). After blooming, allow it a resting period of about two months.

Crab Cactus

POPULAR NAMES: **Prickly Pear, Tuna, Cholla, Opuntia**
SCIENTIFIC NAME: *Opuntia microdasys* var. *albispina*
FAMILY: *Cactaceae* (Cactus)

The original form, called Golden Opuntia because
of its yellow *glochids* (barbed bristles) hails from
Mexico. The white-bristled variety illustrated is
called Polka Dots. Another variety has reddish-
brown glochids. The blossoms of *Opuntia microdasys*
are yellow or, less often, tinged with red.
CARE: As house plants, most Opuntias do not
bloom. The interesting shape of the plant and the
pretty glochids are decorative enough, without
flowers. Only by growing them in the garden in
summer can they be made to bloom, in cool
climates. In summer, they require abundant
warmth and sun and plentiful watering; in winter,
however, they should be kept dry in a cool place
(6 to 8° C or 43 to 46° F).

Prickly Pear

POPULAR NAME: **Tom Thumb Cactus**
SCIENTIFIC NAME: *Parodia chrysacanthion*
FAMILY: *Cactaceae* (Cactus)

This pretty Cactus comes from northern Argentina; it grows small and for that reason is especially good for house plant culture. Similar genera are the Barrel Cacti *(Echinocactus, Ferocactus)*, Chin Cacti *(Gymnocalycium)*, Bale Cacti *(Notocactus)*, and Pincushion Cacti *(Thelocactus)* among others. They bloom at any time from spring to autumn, depending on the species.

CACTUS FAMILY CARE

Cacti are among the best-liked house plants because they are basically undemanding and they delight the eye with their bizarre shapes as well as with their lovely blossoms. Their care is much simpler than that of orchids, for instance. Two main misconceptions, however, lead to many a failure in the care of cacti. During their period of growth, their need for water is easily underestimated; and during their winter resting period, they are often kept too warm. Nearly all cacti love the open sun in summer. Leaf cactus such as the Christmas Cactus and Phyllocactus (Epiphyllum), on the contrary, are damaged by it. Being forest plants, they should be kept in a place that is open-shade to shaded. They go through a less pro-

Tom Thumb Cactus

nounced resting period than the cacti from arid
regions and have a greater need for water. It is
important to water cacti with soft water and to

use a fertilizer that is low in nitrogen. It goes without saying that they are hardly watered at all during their resting period. Cacti that grow in the ground should be wintered over at a temperature range of about 6 to 10° C or 43 to 50° F, while the epiphytic leaf cacti should be kept warmer (about 15° C or 59°F) before blooming and during their resting period, which follows blooming. For those seriously interested in cacti, consultation of the wide range of special literature devoted to this subject is recommended.

POPULAR NAMES: **Epiphyllum, Phyllocactus, Orchid Cactus**
SCIENTIFIC NAME: *Epiphyllum x hybridus (Phyllocactus x hybridus)*
FAMILY: *Cactaceae* (Cactus)

These handsome, large-flowered, leaf cacti are cross-breeds of various epiphytic genera such as *Epiphyllum* and *Nopalxochia* with terrestrial (rooted in soil) cacti such as *Selenicereus* and *Heliocereus*. The flowers range from red through pink, yellowish, and white to blue. Hybridization of the terrestrial cacti with epiphytes produces a strain that can thrive in ordinary garden mould. These cacti bloom in the summer and are cared for the same as the Christmas Cactus. They need two resting periods!

Epiphyllum

POPULAR NAME: **Spiny Mammillaria**
SCIENTIFIC NAME: *Mammillaria spinossima*
FAMILY: *Cactaceae* (Cactus)

The genus Mammillaria offers the cactus fancier an abundance of fine, small, blossoming plants. The species illustrated here hails from central Mexico. Most *Mammillaria* bloom between midwinter and early autumn, but some species bloom in early winter.

Spiny Mammillaria

SCIENTIFIC NAME: *Mammillaria camptotricha, Pseudo-mammillaria camptotricha, Dolichothele camptrotricha*
FAMILY: *Cactaceae* (Cactus)

By whatever scientific name this Mexican cactus is called, it is still closely related to the genus *Mammillaria*. The long, ivory-tinted spines are truly decorative. *Mammillaria camptotricha* is a willing blossomer. The white flowers bloom in late summer.

Bird's Nest Cactus

POPULAR NAMES: **Living Granite, Living Stone**
SCIENTIFIC NAME: *Pleiospilos nelii*
FAMILY: *Aizoaceae* (Fig-Marigold)

The succulent leaves of this South African plant resemble the stones among which they grow naturally, hence the name Living Stone. Not until it bursts into bloom does the plant really look like a member of the Vegetable Kingdom. In the growing season (late spring to early summer) *Pleiospilos* must be given a fair amount of water but in the blooming season that follows immediately thereafter (mid-summer into autumn), the plants should be kept quite dry. During the winter resting period, they may once again be watered.

CARE OF FIG-MARIGOLDS

The Fig-Marigolds are outstandingly adapted to living in the full blaze of sunlight that drenches the African steppes. *Lampranthus* has succulent leaves, *Faucaria* has, in addition, a nearly stemless growth. *Lithops* and *Pleiospilos*—called Living Stones—are extremely succulent and highly adapted to the stony environment. Even in summer they all need only a moderate amount of water—drenching dampness is fatal to them. Above all, the highly succulent Fig-Marigolds are charming plants that take up but little room.

Living Granite

Many thrive and bloom easily without giving much trouble. *Lampranthus* grows bushy and is rather spreading. It is possible to form out a most interesting collection of Fig-Marigold plants in the least amount of room. In winter, move them into a bright, cool and dry place (10° C or 50° F). Do not water during their resting period.

POPULAR NAME: **Ice Carnation**
SCIENTIFIC NAME: *Lampranthus blandus*
FAMILY: *Aizoaceae* (Fig-Marigold)

These Fig-Marigolds are bushy plants with more or less succulent leaves. In summer they require as warm a location as possible, and at that time of year, assuming a suitable place is available, the plant can be moved out into the open. The homeland of the species illustrated here is the Cape region of South Africa.

Ice Carnation

POPULAR NAME: **Tiger Jaws**
SCIENTIFIC NAME: *Faucaria hybrida*
FAMILY: *Aizoaceae* (Fig-Marigold)

Like the other plants of their group, the different species of the genus *Faucaria* hail from the South African Cape country. Their blooming season ranges from late summer to late autumn; the growing season from late spring to the end of the blooming season. Tiger Jaw *(Faucaria tigrina)* and Cat's Chops *(Faucaria felina)* are both popular and owe their names to the resemblance of their toothed leaves to the open mouths of cats. They are cared for like *Lithops* and *Pleiospilos*.

Tiger Jaws

POPULAR NAMES: **Stone Face, Living Stone**
SCIENTIFIC NAME: *Lithops salicola*
FAMILY: *Aizoaceae* (Fig-Marigold)

Except during the blooming season, this flower resembles a flint pebble more than a plant. The various *Lithops* species are told apart more by the patterns of the "windows" on the upper side of the leaf, areas of yellow and greenish grey, than by the blossoms. The growing season for Lithops species ranges from late spring to late autumn, the blooming season from mid-summer to late autumn.

Stone Face

This dwarf pepper hails from Brazil. The plant illustrated is not the green-leaved original species but the cultivated form, "Variegata," with especially beautiful, green-and-white patterned leaves.

CARE: The Peperomia should be placed in a bright, warm location in summer, but not exposed to the direct rays of the sun. In winter, on the contrary, it should be in as bright and sunny a place as possible. At this time, a suitable temperature is 16 to 18° C or 61 to 64° F. In summer, but not in winter, the plant needs high humidity. However, it must not be watered too much. The dwarf pepper blooms from late spring to early autumn, but its real value in the eyes of the flower fancier lies in its beautiful leaves.

Peperomia

POPULAR NAMES: **Mignonette Peperomia, Mignonette Dwarf Pepper**

SCIENTIFIC NAME: *Peperomia resedaeflora*

FAMILY: *Piperaceae* (Pepper)

Peperomia resedaeflora comes from Colombia and closely resembles other dwarf pepper species. The special feature of this peperomia is its fragrant blossoms, but even without blossoms, it is very appealing, with its downy, red-veined, quilted leaves. The blooming season lasts from spring to autumn.

CARE: In summer, it should be placed in a warm location in open shade, and must be protected from the midday sun. The humidity must be kept high, but the plant should not be soaked, as it is vulnerable to stem-rot. Watering is best achieved by spraying. In winter, the plant must not be allowed to get too cold; the temperature should not drop below 16° C or 61° F.

Mignonette Peperomia

POPULAR NAMES: **Magnolia-Leaved Dwarf Pepper,**
   Baby Rubber Plant
SCIENTIFIC NAME: *Peperomia obtusifolia (Peperomia magnoliaefolia)*
FAMILY: *Piperaceae* (Pepper)

This dwarf pepper with fleshy leaves from tropical America grows taller than most of its relatives. Especially popular is the variety illustrated, "Variegata," with green and cream leaves.
CARE: Its care is similar to that of the two other pepper plants described here. The Magnolia-Leaved Dwarf Pepper likes a relatively high humidity and responds to regular spraying with lukewarm rain water during its season of growth. All *Peperomia* species are dwellers in the tropical forests of South America. This explains their preference for warmth, open shade, and high humidity.

Magnolia-Leaved Dwarf Pepper

POPULAR NAME: **Camellia**
SCIENTIFIC NAME: *Camellia japonica (Thea japonica)*
FAMILY: *Theaceae* (Tea)

Of the many cultivated forms of the Camellia once available on the market, only a few are found today, mostly forms with double red, white, red and white, or cream blossoms. The homelands of the wild variety are Japan, Korea and northern China, where it grows as a tree to a height of 15 metres (50 feet).

CARE: The blooming season is in autumn and winter. The winter blooming season of the Camellia must not mislead you into keeping it in a heated room. It cannot stand more than 15 to 16° C or 59 to 61° F. Changing its location and providing too little moisture will lead to dropping of the flower buds. After blooming, it must be kept in a cooler place. In summer, the Camellia thrives best in a shady place in the open. During the growing and blooming season, it requires high humidity and plentiful watering.

Camellia

POPULAR NAME: **Echeveria**
SCIENTIFIC NAME: *Echeveria setosa*
FAMILY: *Crassulaceae* (Orpine)

The Echeveria comes from Mexico. The plant consists of a rosette of fleshy leaves from which a flower stalk emerges, tipped by orange, red or white blossoms.

CARE: In summer the plant can be kept in the house, or even better, in a sheltered, warm place in the open. Sunlight does not harm it, but it must be protected from too much rain. The blooming season of *Echeveria setosa* extends from spring to summer, but many *Echeveria* species bloom in winter. It should winter over in a cool place (6 to 10° C or 43 to 50° F) and should not be watered any more. The winter blooming types are kept somewhat warmer in winter (about 10° C or 50° F) than the plants blooming in spring and summer.

Echeveria

SCIENTIFIC NAME: *Kalanchoe diagremontianum, Bryophyllum diagremontianum*

FAMILY: *Crassulaceae* (Orpine)

This Kalanchoe, like many of its relatives, is a native of Madagascar. The vegetative buds on the edges of the fleshy leaves are what give this plant its special appeal. Arrayed along the leaf edges, tiny plants develop, complete with tiny roots. These plantlets drop off, take root in the soil and soon grow up into independent plants. The grey-violet, bell-shaped, blossoms are also very pretty.

CARE: In summer, this Kalanchoe should be kept where it is bright and warm, and watered only moderately. It can also be kept in a suitable place in the open. In winter, keep it dry and cool (6 to 10° C or 43 to 50° F).

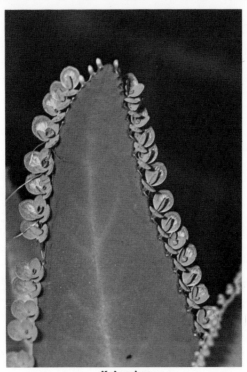

Kalanchoe

Crassulas (Jade Plants) are very popular house plants from South Africa, where they grow to 3 metres (10 feet) high. In the house, they may in the course of years grow into a stately little tree with a thick trunk and fleshy leaves. Very similar to *Crassula portulacea* are *Crassula arborescens* and *C. obliqua*. *Crassula portulacea* blooms in winter, producing small clusters of white or creamy blossoms. When cultivated as a house plant, however, it rarely blooms. Other Crassula species—for instance, *Crassula lactea* (white) and *Crassula falcata* (red)—are admired for their striking blossoms.

CARE: In summer, the plant can be grown in a sunny location in the open. In winter, it needs a cool, bright location where the temperature does not exceed 15° C or 59° F. Water moderately in summer, still less in winter.

Crassula

POPULAR NAMES: **Christmas Kalanchoe, Flaming Katy**
SCIENTIFIC NAME: *Kalanchoe blossfeldiana*
FAMILY: *Crassulaceae* (Orpine)

This succulent (fleshy-leaved) plant, a native of the
mountains of Madagascar, is one of the most
popular for the home, as indicated by the great
number under cultivation. Most plants bear red
blossoms (some forms bear white and yellow) in
almost every season of the year. The blooming
season of the wild variety occurs in spring and
early summer

CARE: In summer, the Kalanchoe should be kept
in an airy, moderately warm place. A spot in the
garden is ideal. Water sparingly—since it is a
succulent, it does not have a great need for water.
Just before and during blooming it should be
watered more plentifully. Fertilize infrequently.
This Kalanchoe must not be kept cooler than 12 to
15° C or 54 to 59° F in winter.

Christmas Kalanchoe

POPULAR NAME: **Strawberry Geranium**
SCIENTIFIC NAME: *Saxifraga sarmentosa*
FAMILY: *Saxifragaceae* (Saxifrage)

The name Saxifrage means "rock breaker" and was given to this family of plants because the plants grow in cracks in rocks where, it was thought, the growing roots caused the rock to break. Owing to the way its runners hang in a beardlike mat, this plant from Japan and China is also called Aaron's Beard (a name bestowed upon certain unrelated plants, also). Its blossoms, white with pink and yellow dots, appear in spring and summer, standing upright. The runners show up best when the plant is hung in a basket.

CARE: It should be placed in open shade, as it is damaged by direct sunlight. During its resting period, from the start of autumn to mid-winter, keep it in a bright, cool place (about 16° C or 61° F). The root-ball must not be permitted to dry out. The cultivated variety, "Tricolor," with green-and-white leaves, requires more warmth than the regular kind.

Strawberry Geranium

POPULAR NAME: **Hydrangea**
SCIENTIFIC NAME: *Hydrangea macrophylla*
FAMILY: *Saxifragaceae* (Saxifrage)

The wild Hydrangeas, like a number of their cultivated varieties, originated in Japan. Hydrangeas bear large clusters of white, pink, red and blue blossoms. In the wild variety, the outer blossoms of the cluster are sterile and larger than the fertile inner ones. Some cultivated varieties, in which all the individual blossoms are large, have lost their ability to bear fruit.

CARE: In summer, when grown as pot plants, Hydrangeas thrive in a bright or open-shaded place outdoors, protected from the direct rays of the sun. At this time of year, they need a great deal of water. In winter, Hydrangeas should be kept cool and dry as well as free from frost, and should be hardly watered at all. Hydrangeas bloom normally from early summer to mid-autumn, although as hothouse plants they bloom in early spring.

Hydrangea

SCIENTIFIC NAME: *Rosa chinensis*
FAMILY: *Rosaceae* (Rose)

The various names above are applied to different varieties of the *Rosa chinensis* species. Long cultivated in its Chinese homeland, it bears double, semi-double, and single blooms in many shades—red, pink, yellow, red-and-white to white. Of the many cultivated varieties, "Minima" (Pygmy Rose), also called "Rouletii," is especially suitable for house plant culture. Indoors it will grow up to 25 or 30 centimetres (10 or 12 inches), but will grow considerably taller when planted outdoors.

CARE: In summer, the China Rose should occupy a bright, airy place but must not be in direct sunlight. Water and fertilize at regular intervals. In winter, keep it in a frost-free, brightly lit place and water it only a little. From mid-winter on, it can become gradually accustomed to higher temperatures. Its normal blooming season extends from spring to mid-autumn.

China Rose

POPULAR NAMES: **Sensitive Plant, Humble Plant, Wild Mimosa**

SCIENTIFIC NAME: *Mimosa pudica*

FAMILY: *Mimosaceae* (Mimosa) or *Leguminosae*, Pea or Pulse Family—some botanists divide the *Leguminosae* into several separate families, including the *Mimosaceae*.

Brazil is the homeland of the Mimosa, which grows wild nowadays in many tropical countries. A remarkable feature of this plant is the unusual sensitivity of the leaves. At the slightest touch or at the approach of darkness, the individual leaflets fold upwards and the entire leaf stalk droops. The pretty purple blossoms open in the summer months. (The yellow Mimosa sold as a cut flower belongs to the related genus *Acacia*.)

CARE: The Mimosa has a rather substantial need for water and in addition requires high humidity. The plant should be kept summer and winter in a warm, bright place. It is not easy to winter Mimosas over in the house and so they are usually cultivated as annuals. The seeds are sown in early spring under glass at a high temperature (20 to 30° C or 68 to 86° F).

Sensitive Plant

POPULAR NAMES: **Otaheite Orange, Dwarf Orange**
SCIENTIFIC NAME: *Citrus x taitensis*
FAMILY: *Rutaceae* (Rue)

The various dwarf citrus trees, like other members of their group, originated in eastern Asia. Accurate information on the parent stock of *Citrus x taitensis* does not exist. A dwarf variety of *Citrus aurantium* (Sour or Seville Orange) resembles it a great deal. The chief attraction of this pretty little tree is the edible, though bitter, fruit. In addition, the fragrant blossoms, which often appear side-by-side with the fruit, are appealing.

CARE: In summer, the Dwarf Oranges should be heavily watered. They thrive best in a sunny, airy location in the open. In winter, water the Dwarf Oranges sparingly and keep them in a cool place (5 to 6° C or 41 to 43° F).

Otaheite Orange

POPULAR NAMES: **Geranium** (of florists), **Storksbill**
SCIENTIFIC NAME: *Pelargonium grandiflorum*
FAMILY: *Geraniaceae* (Geranium)

The ancestors of the horticultural Geranium are very similar to *Pelargonium grandiflorum, Pelargonium cucullatum,* and *Pelargonium cordatum,* all from South Africa. The related genus *Geranium* includes the crane's-bill and various other plants which do not closely resemble the florist's Geranium. These Pelargoniums come in shades of pink, white and deep red, and are somewhat more sensitive than the bedding Geranium, *Pelargonium zonale.* Their blooming period extends from spring until autumn.

CARE: They should be placed where it is bright and airy, but must be protected from direct sun and rain. They do best in the open in summer, or on the sill of an open window. In summer, they must be abundantly watered, but in winter not at all or only very slightly. The wintering-over temperature should be 8 to 12° C or 46 to 54° F.

Geranium

POPULAR NAMES: **Zonal Geranium, Zonal Pelargonium**
SCIENTIFIC NAME: *Pelargonium zonale*
FAMILY: *Geraniaceae* (Geranium)

Of the South African ancestors of the hybrids cultivated nowadays, *Pelargonium zonale*, the bedding Geranium, is the most important. These Geraniums come red, white, pink, salmon and orange. In summer, the Zonal Pelargonium is at its best in the open. It is one of the sturdiest terrace and house plants and withstands the direct sun very well.

CARE: In summer, *Pelargonium zonale* hybrids need rather a lot of water, while during the cold part of the year they should be allowed to go practically unwatered. They should winter over in a place that is cool yet free from frost (5 to 8° C or 41 to 46° F). In the house, they bloom almost the whole year round, in the open from spring to autumn. They can easily be propagated by cuttings rooted in moist sand. Also popular are the ivy-leaved hanging geraniums *(Pelargonium peltatum)*.

Zonal Geranium

POPULAR NAMES: **Busy Lizzie, Touch-Me-Not, Snapweed**
SCIENTIFIC NAME: *Impatiens walleriana*
FAMILY: *Balsaminaceae* (Balsam)

The mountains of tropical East Africa are the original home of the Busy Lizzie, whose cultivated varieties now bear blossoms in a range of hues from white to fiery scarlet, set off by purplish-bronze foliage. They bloom practically the whole year through.

CARE: Busy Lizzies like a bright but not too warm location and should be only moderately watered and fertilized. They can also be taken out on the terrace in the summer. The range of wintering-over temperature is 15 to 18° C or 59 to 64° F. Although a perennial, the Busy Lizzie is mostly cultivated as an annual plant, since old plants become straggly and scrawny in appearance.

Busy Lizzie

POPULAR NAMES: **Chenille Plant, Foxtails, Red Hot
Cat Tail**
SCIENTIFIC NAME: *Acalypha hispida (Acalypha sanderi)*
FAMILY: *Euphorbiaceae* (Spurge)

The actual homeland of *Acalypha hispida*, nowadays
a popular garden plant in many tropical countries,
is not known for certain. It probably came originally from somewhere in India. In addition to
the red-flowered wild form there is also a creamy-
white cultivated variety. Other *Acalypha* species,
such as *Acalypha wilkesiana* with variegated leaves,
have inconspicuous blooms, but are esteemed for
their ornamental leaves.

CARE: The Chenille Plant likes a moist, warm and
sunny location and in summer should be sprinkled
often. Winter temperature must not drop below
16° C or 61° F. The plant's need for water in
winter varies, depending on the surrounding
temperature. The blooming season of *Acalypha
hispida* extends from late spring to mid-autumn
and sometimes lasts still farther on into the winter.

Chenille Plant

POPULAR NAME: **Poinsettia**

SCIENTIFIC NAME: *Euphorbia pulcherrima (Poinsettia pulcherrima)*

FAMILY: *Euphorbiaceae* (Spurge)

In its homeland of tropical Mexico and Central America, the Poinsettia grows from 3 to 4 metres high (10 to 13 feet). The blossoms are small and unassuming; and, it is the vivid, red involucre that make it a highly prized house plant. In addition to the red variety, there are also cultivated varieties with whitish and pink involucres. In the northern hemisphere, the principal blooming season of the Poinsettia falls in the months of December and January, hence it is a popular Christmas plant. It is sometimes called the Short-Day Plant because it does not bloom until the days become short.

CARE: In summer, it thrives well in an open-shaded place outdoors. Its need for water is rather heavy; the root-balls must not be allowed to dry out. Kept in the house, it finds a well lit location with high humidity most suitable. In its resting period, after blooming, it should not be watered until early summer and after that very sparingly. *The milky juice of the Poinsettia is poisonous to taste.*

Poinsettia

POPULAR NAME: **Crown of Thorns**
SCIENTIFIC NAME: *Euphorbia milii (Euphorbia splendens)*
FAMILY: *Euphorbiaceae* (Spurge)

This spiny, climbing spurge from Madagascar bears clusters of charming salmon-pink, flower-like bracts. The blooming season is normally during the months of early spring. It is remarkably resistant to drought.

CARE: The Crown of Thorns should be kept in a bright, sunny location. Do not water often in summer but give it plenty when you do. During its resting period—about early autumn to mid-winter, give it practically no water at all. During this time, the plant should be kept cool (about 10 to 15° C or 50 to 59° F). Standing water is deadly to the Crown of Thorns, so make sure the pot has good drainage.

Crown of Thorns

POPULAR NAMES: **Croton, Brilliantissimum**
SCIENTIFIC NAME: *Codiaeum variegatum* var. *pictum*
FAMILY: *Euphorbiaceae* (Spurge)

Codiaeum is an evergreen shrub from southern India, Ceylon and Indonesia. Its leaves vary widely in size, shape and pattern. They may be mixtures of several shades—from white, through green, yellow, red and brown to black. As with so many foliage plants, the blossoms are inconspicuous.

CARE: Crotons are not easy to care for. Even during the winter resting period they need a lot of warmth, good light and high humidity. The temperature should not be allowed to drop below 16° C or 61° F. The Croton should be in a bright place but protected from direct sunlight. However, if it is in too dark a place, the gaily patterned leaves may turn plain green.

Croton

POPULAR NAME: **Bottle Brush**

SCIENTIFIC NAME: *Callistemon citrinus (Callistemon lanceolatus)*

FAMILY: *Myrtaceae* (Myrtle)

The Bottle Brush—its home is Australia—can be kept in the open during the summer, in an airy, sunny location. It grows up to 3 metres (10 feet) high, though it can be kept as a small house plant and will still bloom. The individual blossoms are small, but their splendid red filaments give the flower spikes an especially impressive look. The blooming season of the Bottle Brush extends as a rule from early summer to early autumn.

CARE: Keep the Bottle Brush cool in winter (5 to 7° C or 41 to 45° F) and, contrary to the usual, water it very little in summer. The plant does best in full sun.

Bottle Brush

POPULAR NAME: **Myrtle**
SCIENTIFIC NAME: *Myrtus communis*
FAMILY: *Myrtaceae* (Myrtle)

The homeland of the Myrtle is the Mediterranean region, where it grows as a shrub 1 to 5 metres high (3 to 16 feet). It is a well known house plant in many lands and a large number of cultivated varieties have been developed. Depending on the species, the fragrant blossoms are white or reddish. There are also varieties with double blossoms. The glossy dark green leaves are aromatic.

CARE: In summer, Myrtle does best in the open in either a semi-shaded or sunny place. It should be heavily watered and sprayed or sprinkled with soft water, but be very careful not to let water stand in the pot. Keep it cool in winter (2 to 6° C or 36 to 43° F) and relatively dry. Also at this time of year it should be in a place that is bright and airy.

Myrtle

POPULAR NAME: **Blue Passion Flower**
SCIENTIFIC NAME: *Passiflora coerulea*
FAMILY *Passifloraceae* (Passion Flower)

Southern Brazil, Paraguay and Argentina are the home of the bright blue, wild forms of this climbing shrub, ancestors of the very large-blossomed cultivated varieties available today in mixtures of purple, blue and white. The cultured variety illustrated here, the "Empress Eugenie," makes a good house plant, while the other varieties are better for outdoor cultivation. The blooming season extends from early summer to mid-autumn.
CARE: In summer, keep the Blue Passion Flower in the house in a brightly lit place protected from direct sunlight. It can also be kept in the open in a protected location. In the summer growing season, it needs a great deal of water, but in the winter only a little. The wintering-over temperature should be between 5 and 10° C or 41 to 50° F. You can raise your own plants from the seeds of the edible Passion Flower fruit, which is on sale in winter in some fruit and vegetable stalls.

Blue Passion Flower

POPULAR NAME: **Red Passion Flower**
SCIENTIFIC NAME: *Passiflora racemosa*
FAMILY: *Passifloraceae* (Passion Flower)

This Red Passion Flower from Brazil is especially beautiful. It grows more slowly than the Blue Passion Flower and therefore is especially suitable for flower pot culture.

CARE: Although it likes warmth, like its blue relative, the Red Passion Flower in proper climatic conditions can be planted outdoors in summer in a protected location. In their care, both species are alike. *Passiflora racemosa*, however, should be wintered over at a somewhat warmer temperature than the blue species. It does best in loose soil that permits a good water run-off.

Red Passion Flower

POPULAR NAME: **Flowering Maple**
SCIENTIFIC NAME: *Abutilon hybridum*
FAMILY: *Malvaceae* (Mallow)

The ancestors of the cultivated varieties of the Flowering Maple are native to Brazil *(Abutilon darwinii)* and Guatemala *(Abutilon striatum)*. There are now varieties with whitish, yellow, red, and red-brown blossoms. In normal cultivation, the blooming season takes place between the middle of spring and the middle of autumn. The varieties of *Abutilon* with variegated leaves have a shorter blooming season, but their white and green leaves provide a very decorative effect. The flowering maple grows more than a metre (39¼ inches) high when cultivated in a pot.

CARE: The Flowering Maple should be kept in a place that is sunny to partly shaded, and if possible, in the open as well. At this time it should be abundantly watered, while in autumn and winter, in the house, it should be watered less. The Flowering Maple should winter over in a bright but cool place (10 to 15° C or 50 to 59° F).

Flowering Maple

POPULAR NAMES: **Rose Mallow, Hibiscus, Japanese Lantern**
SCIENTIFIC NAME: *Hibiscus schizopetalus*
FAMILY: *Malvaceae* (Mallow)

Tropical East Africa is the homeland of this especially beautiful species of Hibiscus, the Rose Mallow genus. It blooms in the northern hemisphere from about February until September. In addition to the wild variety, there are numerous hybrids, which are popular as garden plants, especially in the tropics and subtropics.

CARE: This Rose Mallow requires more warmth than *Hibiscus rosa-sinensis* (see page 96)—but this is no disadvantage for house plant culture in the winter. In summer, it should be in an airy, sunny place, and if placed in the open, the location should also be a protected one. In summer, water plentifully, but in winter, depending on how cool the plant is kept, watering can be somewhat reduced. *Hibiscus schizopetalus* spreads out more than does *Hibiscus rosa-sinensis*, and thus requires more room.

Rose Mallow

SCIENTIFIC NAME: *Hibiscus rosa-sinensis* var. *Calleri*
FAMILY: *Malvaceae* (Mallow)

This large-blossomed, yellow, cultured variety, "*Lateritia*," is a good example of the multiplicity of garden varieties that have been bred from the wild species of Rose Mallow. There are double and single blossoms—white, pink, yellow, cream and various combinations of these. The single blossoms resembling those of the wild species are especially elegant.

CARE: The principal blooming season of the Hibiscus stretches from spring into autumn. During this time it requires a great deal of water and an airy, sunny-to-half-shaded location with high humidity. It also thrives well in a sheltered place in the open. It can be wintered over at temperatures of 12 to 15° C or 54 to 59° F or even warmer.

Yellow Rose-of-China

POPULAR NAMES: **Red Rose-of-China, Chinese Red Hibiscus**

SCIENTIFIC NAME: *Hibiscus rosa-sinensis* var. *Van Houttei*

FAMILY: *Malvaceae* (Mallow)

The single red blossoms of this cultivated variety of Hibiscus are the closest to those of the wild species. Unfortunately, Hibiscus flowers remain open only one day, or two days at the most. A sturdy Rose-of-China bush, however, has a high blooming potential, which compensates quite well for the short life of the individual blossoms. The variety *Cooperi* (not shown) is distinguished from other strains by its white-edged, pink and carmine, checkered leaves. Its small scarlet blossoms are inconspicuous.

CARE: Similar to var. *Calleri*.

Red Rose-of-China

POPULAR NAME: **Credner's Begonia**
SCIENTIFIC NAME: *Begonia x credneri*
FAMILY: *Begoniaceae* (Begonia)

This hybrid is a cross between two Brazilian wild species—*Begonia metallica* and *Begonia scharffiana*. The result is a compact plant which blooms almost the whole year through. It is true that the pink blossoms are smaller than those of many other Begonias, but the leaves alone give a decorative effect.

CARE: Credner's Begonia should be kept the year round in the house in a bright, lightly shaded location. In summer, water regularly. Water less during the resting period. Fertilize at intervals of two weeks. The most suitable temperatures for these Begonias in winter are between 15 and 20° C or 59 to 68° F.

Credner's Begonia

POPULAR NAMES: **Rex Begonia, Beefsteak Geranium**
SCIENTIFIC NAME: *Begonia x rex*
FAMILY: *Begoniaceae* (Begonia)

Begonia rex, from the Indian state of Assam, is the only one of the species from which the so-called *rex-cultorum* hybrids of horticulture, have been bred. The original species is hardly ever found on the market. In its place are numerous varieties prized for their beautiful leaves. The green, red, violet, bronze, maroon and silvery tones of the leaves lend a great deal of charm to these plants. The blossoms are inconspicuous.

CARE: The Rex Begonia cannot stand direct sunlight; it should be located in a semi-shaded place, with high humidity. In winter, the temperature should not drop below 16° C or 61° F, and for this reason, the plant should be kept in a heated room. Water sparingly during the winter resting period, but the earth in the pot must not be allowed to dry out. During this time, the plant drops all of its leaves.

Rex Begonia

POPULAR NAME: **Elatior Begonia**
SCIENTIFIC NAME: *Begonia x elatior*
FAMILY: *Begoniaceae* (Begonia)

The group of Elatior Begonias consists of various hybrids. The most important parent plants are *Begonia socotrana,* from the island of Socotra in the Indian Ocean, and *Begonia x tuberhybrida,* the Tuberous Begonia, a crossing of several South American species. The large red, yellow, orange or white blossoms appear in the autumn or in the middle of winter.

CARE: Unfortunately, these beautiful Begonias are very difficult to care for. They must not be allowed to get too warm (only about 12° C or 54° F); they are sensitive to drafts, require high humidity, but should not be sprayed or kept too wet. Therefore, they are best purchased as blooming plants without trying to winter them over. The similar *Begonia semperflorens* varieties are less delicate, but have smaller blossoms.

Elatior Begonia

POPULAR NAMES: **African Hemp, African Linden, Sparmannia**

SCIENTIFIC NAME: *Sparmannia africana*

FAMILY: *Tiliaceae* (Linden)

The African Hemp, a shrub from the Cape country of South Africa, is liked for its large pale-green, hairy leaves as well as for its pretty white and yellow blossoms.

CARE: It prefers a bright, airy location, out of the direct rays of the sun. In summer, it can be kept out of doors or in an open window. It should be watered throughout the year. In winter, it should be kept cooler (5 to 12° C or 41 to 54° F), and watered somewhat less. The blossoms appear in the spring, but they do not develop if the plant has not had an adequate autumn and winter resting period, with cooler temperatures.

African Hemp

POPULAR NAME: **English Ivy**
SCIENTIFIC NAME: *Hedera helix*
FAMILY: *Araliaceae* (Aralia or Ginseng)

The familiar English Ivy actually comes from a wide range in Europe, Asia and North Africa, and has given rise to a large number of horticultural varieties. The dwarf varieties are suitable for pot culture. Especially popular are the kinds having variegated leaves, such as "Argenteo-Variegata," which is mottled with white (illustrated).

CARE: In summer, ivy should be in semi-shade—it even grows in dark corners. It should not be watered too heavily, but the leaves can be sprinkled often. Ivy should be regularly fertilized. It can winter over either in the cold (2 to 3° C or 36 to 38° F), or in a heated room. *English Ivy is poisonous if eaten.*

English Ivy

POPULAR NAME: **Fuchsia**
SCIENTIFIC NAME: *Fuchsia x hybrida*
FAMILY: *Onagraceae* (Evening Primrose)

The original forms of the present-day Fuchsia
hybrids come from South and Central America.
Fuchsias have woody stems and bell-shaped,
hanging blossoms, typically with scarlet sepals and
pink, crimson or magenta petals, but also in
combinations of pink, white and purple.
CARE: In summer, Fuchsia hybrids should be kept
in a bright, semi-shaded place with high humidity,
whether out of doors or on a terrace, but they
must be protected from the direct sun. Fuchsias
need heavy watering in the summer. In winter,
they should be kept in a bright, cool place (3 to
10° C or 38 to 50° F) and should be watered
hardly at all. After the close of their resting period,
beginning with spring, they can be re-potted and
put in a warmer place. The blossoms appear
between mid-spring and mid-autumn.

Fuchsia

POPULAR NAMES: **Medinilla, Rose Grape**
SCIENTIFIC NAME: *Medinilla magnifica*
FAMILY: *Melastomaceae* (Melastoma)

The Medinilla, which comes from Java and the Philippines, is a shrubby plant with long, leathery leaves and striking clusters of purplish-red flowers set in huge pink bracts.

CARE: A warmth-loving plant, it should be kept warm even in winter (15 to 20° C or 59 to 68° F). However, it does not like direct sunlight and so must be kept in a semi-shaded location. Since the Medinilla needs high humidity in order to thrive, it must be sprinkled often. In the summer growing season, water and fertilize it frequently. The blossoms of the Medinilla, in normal culture, open in the middle of spring, and stay open until early summer. A winter resting period with slightly lower temperature and less watering than in summer will stimulate the formation of the blossoms.

Medinilla

POPULAR NAMES: **Aucuba, Gold Dust**
SCIENTIFIC NAME: *Aucuba japonica*
FAMILY: *Cornaceae* (Dogwood)

The leaves of the wild variety of this evergreen bush from Japan are green, while the leaves of many cultivated forms are wonderfully patterned with yellow or red specks and blotches.

CARE: The Aucuba makes a sturdy house plant that should be kept in a place both light and airy, but protected from direct sunlight and excessive warmth. In summer, it needs plenty of water, including sprinkling. During the winter resting period, keep the Aucuba in a bright, cool place (3 to 5° C or 38 to 41° F), and give it very little water. The purplish blossoms appear in early summer, but they are not very conspicuous. As a house plant, the Aucuba reaches the not inconsiderable height of about 2 metres (6½ feet).

Aucuba

POPULAR NAMES: **Madagascar Jasmine, Stephanotis**
SCIENTIFIC NAME: *Stephanotis floribunda*
FAMILY: *Asclepiadaceae* (Milkweed)

Madagascar is the homeland of this well liked woody vine, which can climb as high as 5 metres (16 feet). With proper care, even young plants will bloom, the fragrant white flowers appearing all through the summer.

CARE: In summer, the Madagascar Jasmine prefers a bright and airy spot, out of the direct sun. At this time of year, it needs a great deal of watering and should frequently be sprinkled or sprayed. During its resting period, from autumn to mid-winter, it should be kept cooler and watered considerably less. The Madagascar Jasmine is a summer-flowering plant, but the blooming season can be extended into the autumn by artificial illumination.

Madagascar Jasmine

POPULAR NAMES: **Wax Plant, Wax Flower**
SCIENTIFIC NAME: *Hoya carnosa*
FAMILY: *Asclepidaceae* (Milkweed)

The Wax Plant is a well liked climbing plant from China and northern Australia. The stems are rubbery and the leaves are thick and waxlike. Its glistening, red-and-pink, waxy blossoms grow in dense heads and emit a pleasant fragrance. The cultured variety, "Variegatum," has yellowish-white, red-edged leaves.

CARE: It should be kept in a warm, bright place, but protected from the direct sun, and should be watered heavily in summer. It winters over best at a temperature of 10 to 14° C or 50 to 57° F. During this time, give it less water. The Wax Plant blooms from spring to mid-autumn. Once the plant has started to bloom, it must not be moved to another location. Moving the plant at this time could seriously affect and even injure development of the blossoms. After the plant has ceased flowering, do not cut off the flower stalks, as new buds will develop on them.

Wax Plant

POPULAR NAMES: **Florists' Cyclamen, Sowbread, Alpine Violet**
SCIENTIFIC NAME: *Cyclamen persicum*
FAMILY: *Primulaceae* (Primrose)

This Cyclamen from the eastern Mediterranean region is the one most often found in florists' shops. In some Mediterranean countries, the tubers are fed to swine, to enhance the taste of the meat, hence the name Sowbread. Blossoms of the wild form are white or red, but there are garden varieties in white, pink, salmon, lilac and combinations of these. They appear between mid-autumn and early spring.

CARE: The Cyclamen should be kept in a semi-shady, airy place, protected from the direct rays of the sun. Give it soft water and take care not to wet the leaves. Excessive heat is harmful—the temperature should not rise above 16° C or 61° F in summer nor 10° C or 50° F in winter. In the warm period of the year, water abundantly; in winter, only moderately. The leaves die off after the blossoms, and in the spring, the new plant springs up from the underground tuber.

Florists' Cyclamen

POPULAR NAME: **Primrose**
SCIENTIFIC NAME: *Primula obconica*
FAMILY: *Primulaceae* (Primrose)

China is the homeland of the most important ancestral stock of the numerous cultivated varieties of the Primrose. Depending on the variety, the globelike clusters of blossoms may be red, white, pink, or lilac. The crisp, bright-green, aromatic leaves are somewhat prickly. The plant is grown as an annual.

CARE: In summer, the Primrose should be kept in semi-shade, in winter in a bright but cool place (8° C or 46° F). The blooming season normally extends from mid-winter to mid-summer, but Primroses that bloom in winter, for Christmas, are also available. This Primrose's need for water is minimal, but take care when watering not to wet the leaves. Some people are allergic to the leaf hairs.

Primrose

POPULAR NAMES: **Gardenia, Cape Jasmine**
SCIENTIFIC NAME: *Gardenia jasminoides*
FAMILY: *Rubiaceae* (Madder)

The Gardenia, a shrub 30 to 180 centimetres high (12 to 72 inches) originated in China. It is a well liked house plant because of its beautiful, fragrant white blossoms, and shiny, dark green leaves.

CARE: As a rule, the blooming season runs from early summer to mid-autumn. In summer, the Gardenia should be kept in a warm, airy place, with plenty of light and humidity. Gardenias prefer a somewhat acid soil, so be careful not to give them water that is strongly alkaline. They should be wintered over at 10 to 15° C or 50 to 59° F. Water sparingly in winter. Gardenias are not difficult to propagate from cuttings. A few similar species from East and South Africa are also suitable for house plants.

Gardenia

POPULAR NAMES: **Ixora, Flame-of-the-Forest**
SCIENTIFIC NAME: *Ixora coccinea*
FAMILY: *Rubiaceae* (Madder)

These magnificent shrubs are native to India and Indonesia, where they grow to a height of 5 metres (16 feet). In addition to the original species, *Ixora coccinea*, there are many cultivated varieties whose exact ancestry is unknown. Ixoras have leathery leaves and dense heads of tube-shaped, scarlet flowers. Since they bloom while still young plants, they are well suited for pot culture. When the plants are moved from the greenhouse into the house, they often lose their blossoms, however.

CARE: The most suitable spot for the Ixora is one that is bright to semi-shady but warm (16 to 26° C or 62 to 86° F). Water frequently in summer, sprinkling and fertilizing at the same time. After blooming, give older plants a resting period under somewhat cooler (10 to 18° C or 50 to 62° F) and drier conditions, and they will bloom again.

Ixora

POPULAR NAME: **Coral Bead Plant**

SCIENTIFIC NAME: *Nertera granadensis (Nertera depressa)*

FAMILY: *Rubiaceae* (Madder)

The Coral Bead Plant hails from the Andes Mountains of South America, as well as from New Zealand and Tasmania. The greenish-white blossoms are inconspicuous—the plant is cultivated rather for its orange-red fruits. The blooming season of the Bead Plant begins some time in mid-spring and the berries appear in mid-summer.

CARE: The Bead Plant likes an airy, semi-shady location and thrives outdoors in summer. It winters over at a temperature range of from 10 to 12° C or 50 to 54° F. The plant should be kept moist throughout the year but not soaking wet. High humidity can be obtained by spraying the air around the plant with water, but avoid spraying water directly on the blossoms. The attractive berries stay on the plant into the winter.

Coral Bead Plant

POPULAR NAMES: **Exacum, Persian Violet, Arabian Gentian**

SCIENTIFIC NAME: *Exacum affine*

FAMILY: *Gentianaceae* (Gentian)

The blue Exacum is a mountain plant from the island of Socotra in the Arabian Sea. The blooming season of this biennial plant comes in the summer and autumn. The cultivated variety, "Atrocoeruleum," is especially beautiful.

CARE: *Exacum affine* likes high humidity and requires regular, light watering throughout the year. In summer, place the plant in an airy, not too warm location; in winter keep it very cool (8° C or 46° F). If you do not want to winter the Exacum over, you can grow new plants from cuttings.

Exacum

POPULAR NAMES: **Coleus, Painted Nettle, Flame Nettle**
SCIENTIFIC NAME: *Coleus x blumei*
FAMILY: *Labiatae* (Mint)

The parent stock of the hybrids grouped under the designation *blumei* come from Java. Since some cultivated varieties already exist there, we do not know exactly which wild species they spring from. The wide range of coloration and patterns in the foliage has made many friends for the Coleus. The light blue blossoms, which flourish from the beginning of summer to mid-autumn, are also appealing.

CARE: Coleus thrives best in a room that is not too warm and in a sunny location. The plant will form a bushy growth if the terminal buds are pinched off. In summer, it can be placed outdoors. At this time of year, water plentifully. In winter, watering should be reduced and the temperature raised somewhat higher (18 to 20° C or 64 to 68° F). It is best to renew the stock of plants each year by raising new plants from cuttings. The cuttings will root readily in water or moist sand.

Coleus

POPULAR NAMES: **Azalea, Rhododendron, Rose Bay**
SCIENTIFIC NAME: *Rhododendron simsii ("Azalea indica")*
FAMILY: *Ericaceae* (Heath)

Rhododendron simsii from China and Formosa is the most important ancestral form of many hybrids. Some kinds have single flowers and others double, in white, pink, red, dark red and mixtures of these. The normal blooming season of the Azalea occurs in the winter months, through early spring, but some varieties flower beyond that period. Even in the autumn florist shops now offer Azalea plants that are still in bloom.

CARE: In summer the Azalea thrives best in a semi-shaded location out of doors or on the sill of an open window. It should be watered only with soft rainwater and should be sprinkled in very warm weather. The fertilizer used must be free of lime. Azaleas should be wintered over in a cool (4 to 10° C or 39 to 50° F), bright place. *Azaleas are poisonous if eaten.*

Azalea

POPULAR NAMES: **Clerodendrum, Glory Bower,**
   Bleeding-Heart Vine
SCIENTIFIC NAME: *Clerodendrum thomsoniae*
FAMILY: *Verbenaceae* (Vervain)

This climbing bush from tropical West Africa and
the Congo Valley climbs to a height of 4 metres
(13 feet). The shiny dark green leaves have a
quilted texture and the clusters of flowers are
spectacular—crimson petals set in snow-white or
pinkish calyxes.
CARE: In summer, it requires a bright, warm
location protected from the raw sun. At this time,
water abundantly and fertilize heavily. In winter,
allow the Clerodendrum a resting period, during
which it is not to be watered any more and the
plant is to be kept in a bright, cool place (10 to
15° C or 50 to 59° F). From mid-winter on,
watering can be resumed gradually. The shrub soon
leafs out again and the lovely blossoms appear in
the spring. A more compact growth of the
Clerodendrum is achieved by cutting it back.

Clerodendrum

POPULAR NAMES: **Lantana, Shrub Verbena, Yellow Sage**
SCIENTIFIC NAME: *Lantana camara*
FAMILY: *Verbenaceae* (Vervain)

The Lantana originated in tropical America and now grows wild in many parts of the tropics. The blossoms on a single plant may be of different shades, since the individual blossoms may change, in the course of time, from pink and yellow to orange and dark red. In addition to the wild species there is a considerable number of similar cultivated varieties.

CARE: In summer the Lantana should be in a sunny and airy location; it can also be kept outdoors. During this time, it should be watered and fertilized abundantly, while in winter watering should be drastically reduced. The wintering-over temperature should not be higher than 8 to 10° C or 46 to 50° F. The Lantana ~an grow to more than 1 metre (39½ inches) high and for this reason must be cut back after blooming if it is to be kept as a small house plant. In the North Temperate Zone, it blooms from May to October. *Don't let children nibble on the Lantana as it is poisonous to the taste.*

Lantana

POPULAR NAME: **Dipladenia**
SCIENTIFIC NAME: *Dipladenia sanderi*
FAMILY: *Apocynaceae* (Dogbane)

The ancestral form of this handsome creeper (up to 2 metres or $6\frac{1}{2}$ feet long), from which most of the present-day varieties on the market are derived, comes from Brazil. The plants have woody stems and small, shiny leaves, with a brownish cast on the underside. The large flowers are pinkish with a yellow interior.

CARE: It requires protection only from direct mid-day sun, especially when the light comes through lenslike window panes. During its season of growth, it requires a great deal of water, but water should never be allowed to stand in the pot. Fertilize about every two weeks. The blooming season of the Dipladenia extends from the middle of spring to late autumn; the individual blossoms last for weeks. After blooming, the Dipladenia should be watered sparingly and kept cool (12 to 15° C or 54 to 59° F). In early spring, water and temperature can be gradually increased.

Dipladenia

POPULAR NAME: **Oleander**
SCIENTIFIC NAME: *Nerium oleander*
FAMILY: *Apocynaceae* (Dogbane)

The Oleander, long a popular tub plant, is a native of the Mediterranean region. In a hot, dry summer, it can be kept outdoors; in rainy years, it will bloom only in a sunny spot in the house. Its blooming season extends from late spring to mid-autumn. In addition to the variety illustrated, there are types of Oleander having white, yellow and double blossoms.

CARE: While the Oleander must have a great deal of warmth and sun in the summer, it should be kept cool during its winter resting period (2 to 10° C or 36 to 50° F). As a shrub or tree, the Oleander attains a height of 3 to 6 metres (10 to 20 feet) and for this reason, when grown as a house plant, it must be regularly cut back in early spring. Only cut back branches which have already flowered, however. During its growing season it requires a great deal of water and fertilizer. Keep away from children and pets—*all parts of the plant are extremely poisonous if eaten.*

Oleander

POPULAR NAMES: **Red Pepper, Capsicum**
SCIENTIFIC NAME: *Capsicum annuum*
FAMILY: *Solanaceae* (Nightshade)

Central and South America are the homelands of the ornamental pepper which is sold for house plant culture as an annual, growing 30 to 60 centimetres high (12 to 24 inches). The Red Pepper blooms all during the summer, but its blossoms are inconspicuous. Not until the splendid red, yellow or violet fruits (peppers) appear does the plant show off to best advantage.

CARE: This plant likes warmth and should be watered heavily with luke-warm water until after the fruits appear. Most plant fanciers, however, buy the Red Pepper plant only after the peppers, its real ornamentation, have already developed. The Red Pepper is easy to propagate by means of seeds.

Red Pepper

POPULAR NAMES: **Brunfelsia, Franciscea**
SCIENTIFIC NAME: *Brunfelsia calycina*
FAMILY: *Solanaceae* (Nightshade)

Several species of these Brazilian shrubs are to be found in florists' shops. Best liked are the varieties with blue and violet blossoms which turn partially pure white while blooming. Some species have a pleasant fragrance, but not the one illustrated.

CARE: Unfortunately, the warmth-loving Brunfelsia is quite sensitive to sudden variations in temperature. Also, it suffers if its earth-ball is allowed to become either too wet or too dry. For this reason, it should be watered regularly but carefully. The Brunfelsia likes a warm, lightly shaded location. Its blooming season extends through the winter into the middle of spring, after which it should be put aside for a short resting period. The real resting period takes place in late autumn and early winter, when the plant should be kept cool (about 15° C or 59° F) and dry.

Brunfelsia

POPULAR NAME: **Jacobinia**
SCIENTIFIC NAME: *Jacobinia pohliana*
FAMILY: *Acanthaceae* (Acanthus)

More often seen than the species illustrated here is the very similar *Jacobinia carnea (Justicia magnifica* and *carnea)*. Jacobinias are prized for their spray-like heads of pink blossoms. Both come from Brazil and are cared for in the same way.

CARE: The Jacobinias are easier to care for than is often supposed. In summer, they can even be kept in a sheltered location outdoors; however, they must be protected from the direct rays of the noonday sun. During the growing period they require a lot of water; the earth-ball must not dry out in the pot. In winter, less water is required. Depending on growing conditions, Jacobinias bloom from the middle of spring until late summer, even until mid-autumn. They should be fertilized once a week during the growing season. They winter over best where it is cool and bright, temperature ranging from 10 to 12° C or 50 to 54° F.

Jacobinia

POPULAR NAME: **Aphelandra**
SCIENTIFIC NAME: *Aphelandra squarrosa*
FAMILY: *Acanthaceae* (Acanthus)

The wild species hails from Brazil. It is no longer found in cultivation as a pure species, though the photograph shows a hybrid that is representative of the most important ancestral side. Both leaves and inflorescence of the Aphelandra are of exceptional beauty. The red-tipped yellow bracts are quite spectacular, and from them emerge the pale yellow flowers (which have not yet appeared in the specimen illustrated).

CARE: The Aphelandra likes warmth and requires a bright but shaded location. It should be watered and fertilized abundantly, and also sprayed with water regularly. After blooming is over, cut the plant back, to make it branch out better, and put it away in a somewhat cooler place. During the winter resting period keep the Aphelandra warm (at least 18° C or 64° F). Reduce watering during this period also. As a rule, the Aphelandra blossoms appear between early spring and early autumn.

Aphelandra

POPULAR NAME: **Shrimp Plant**
SCIENTIFIC NAME: *Beloperone guttata*
FAMILY: *Acanthaceae* (Acanthus)

This ornamental shrub from Mexico blooms practically the whole year through. The drooping flower stalks bear reddish-brown bracts, which are more striking than the white blossoms.

CARE: The Shrimp Plant prefers a warm location. The more light and air it receives, the more intense the coloration of the bracts. However, it must be protected from the glare of direct summer sunlight. Water the plant plentifully in summer and sparingly in its winter resting period. In winter, it requires a temperature of only about 12 to 15° C or 54 to 59° F. Even if the plant is not given its normal winter resting period, it will continue to bloom.

Shrimp Plant

POPULAR NAME: **Crossandra**
SCIENTIFIC NAME: *Crossandra infundibuliformis*
FAMILY: *Acanthaceae* (Acanthus)

Crossandra is from India, unlike most of the Acanthus species commonly seen as house plants, which are from South America. The flowers are an attractive salmon pink and even when the Crossandra is not in bloom, it still has a very striking appearance owing to its waxy, dark green leaves. The blooming season lasts for a long time— from late winter to late autumn. With proper care it can be extended even further on into the winter. CARE: The Crossandra has no distinct resting period, but in winter should be kept warm (18 to 20° C or 64 to 68° F). The root-ball must not be permitted to dry out. At the height of its growing season—mid-winter to late summer—it should be fertilized weekly.

Crossandra

POPULAR NAMES: **Black-Eyed Susan, Clock Vine, Thunbergia**

SCIENTIFIC NAME: *Thunbergia alata*

FAMILY: *Acanthaceae* (Acanthus)

This climbing plant (2 metres or 6½ feet high) from southeast Africa grows wild today in practically all tropical countries. (It is not related to the familiar wild Black-eyed Susan of North America, which belongs to the genus *Rudbeckia*.) The blossoms of the cultivated forms range from white through yellow and orange to brownish-orange. The blooming season extends from early summer to mid-autumn.

CARE: This plant requires a warm, sunny location; in summer it does well in sheltered places in the open. It requires heavy watering. The Black-Eyed Susan is usually cultivated as an annual plant; but it can be wintered over in a cool, bright place (10 to 12° C or 50 to 54° F). Seeds for new plants can be sown at the end of winter, and the new plants will start blooming 15 weeks later.

Black-Eyed Susan

Acanthus ■ 157

POPULAR NAMES: **Smithiantha, Naegelia, Temple Bells**
SCIENTIFIC NAME: *Smithiantha cinnabarina*
FAMILY: *Gesneriaceae* (Gesneria)

Numerous cultivated varieties and hybrids from crossings with other species of the genus have replaced the original Mexican variety of Smithiantha in horticulture. The plants grow 30 to 60 centimetres (12 to 24 inches) high and are admired for both their scarlet blossoms and their velvety reddish leaves.

CARE: The direct rays of the sun are to be avoided. After the plant has bloomed, it should still be watered a little so that the underground rhizomes can develop. Then it should be given a rest for 3 months, during which time no water is needed. During their resting period, the rhizomes should remain potted and at a temperature of 8 to 10° C or 46 to 50° F.

Smithiantha

POPULAR NAME: **Achimenes**
SCIENTIFIC NAME: *Achimenes hybrida*
FAMILY: *Gesneriaceae* (Gesneria)

The parent plants of all cultivated forms of Achimenes come from Mexico and Central America. Today, almost all forms under cultivation are hybrids. Achimenes bloom throughout the whole summer, and come in varieties having purple, blue-violet, red, cream or white blossoms.

CARE: The plants should be kept in a bright, warm place but protected from the direct rays of the sun. They require only an average amount of water and fertilizer. However, be sure that the water is free of lime and that only organic fertilizer is used. After blooming, the plant dies down to the roots. The small rhizomes should be dried and stored at a temperature range of 14 to 18° C or 57 to 64° F until they are planted again in the spring.

Achimenes

POPULAR NAMES: **Aeschynanthus, Trichosporum**
SCIENTIFIC NAME: *Aeschynanthus lobbianus (Tricho-*
sporum lobbianum)
FAMILY: *Gesneriaceae* (Gesneria)

Species of the genus *Aeschynanthus (Trichosporum)*
are dwellers of the rain forests of tropical Asia,
while the representatives of the quite similar genus
Columnea inhabit the jungles of tropical America.
Both genera include beautifully blooming, hanging
and climbing plants, which for the most part live
epiphytically.
CARE: Unfortunately, the care of many of the
species is not easy, particularly since they require
high humidity. In spite of this, the plants should
not be watered too abundantly and, like all
Gesneria plants, need soft water. Fertilize at about
10-day intervals. The plant should be kept in a
warm but shady place. The blooming season
occurs in spring and summer. In winter, reduce
watering, and keep at a temperature of 15 to
20° C or 59 to 68° F.

Aeschynanthus

POPULAR NAMES: **Gloxinia, Sinningia**
SCIENTIFIC NAME: *Sinningia hybrida*
FAMILY: *Gesneriaceae* (Gesneria)

The wild Gloxinias hail from the tropical forests of South America. Closely related to the true Gloxinias, the Sinningias are commonly called Gloxinias by florists and horticulturists. The blooming season extends from the middle of spring to mid-summer.

CARE: The Gloxinia likes a bright, warm location with humidity not too low. However, direct exposure to the sun is undesirable. The plant should be sprayed regularly with luke-warm, soft water and moderately watered at soil level. After the plant blooms, watering can be reduced. When the leaves fall off, the corm (bulblike root) can be allowed to winter over in the pot at a temperature of 10 to 15° C or 50 to 59° F, but should not be allowed to dry out completely.

Gloxinia

POPULAR NAME: **Cape Primrose**
SCIENTIFIC NAME: *Streptocarpus rexii*.
FAMILY: *Gesneriaceae* (Gesneria)

The wild species of *Streptocarpus rexii,* which is the most important parent stock of the numerous *Streptocarpus* hybrids, hails from South Africa. The illustrated variety strongly resembles the wild species, while the white, red and lilac hybrids show considerable deviation. The resemblance to African violets (see page 169) is not accidental—they are related.

CARE: The Cape Primrose likes a bright but semi-shaded location out of the direct sun. Always water abundantly with soft, luke-warm water. Keep the plant in a cool place in winter (10 to 12° C or 50 to 54° F). Propagation can be done by means of cuttings. The Cape Primrose blooms throughout the entire summer.

Cape Primrose

POPULAR NAMES: **African Violet, Usambara Violet**
SCIENTIFIC NAME: *Saintpaulia ionantha*
FAMILY: *Gesneriaceae* (Gesneria)

The African Violet originally came from the tropical virgin forest of the Usambara Mountains in Tanzania, East Africa. It loves warmth, but not direct sunlight. By selective breeding, the blossoms have become enlarged and now white, pink and red cultured varieties are found along with the original blue ones. The plant flowers throughout the whole year, with autumn and spring the times of greatest blooming.

CARE: The African Violet needs only a moderate amount of water, but only soft water should be used. The plants should be sprinkled or sprayed, as well as watered at soil level. After blooming, they should be put in a cooler place where they can winter over at about 12 to 18° C or 54 to 64° F. They can be propagated by dividing the healthier plants and by cuttings.

African Violet

POPULAR NAMES: **Gesneria, Cardinal Flower**
SCIENTIFIC NAME: *Rechtsteineria cardinalis (Corytholoma cardinalis, Gesneria cardinalis)*
FAMILY: *Gesneriaceae* (Gesneria)

Called Gesneria by florists, this tropical Brazilian flower is a close relative of the true Gesneria. The tube-shaped flowers are bright red and the velvety leaves are a vivid green.

CARE: The Gesneria should be kept in a bright and warm place, but sheltered from the direct rays of the sun. It requires abundant watering and a humid atmosphere—it will be injured by air that is too dry. The part of the Gesneria above ground dies down in the autumn. Therefore, gradually reduce the quantity of water after the plant has bloomed and finally put the plant away in a warm, dry place and let the tubers winter over there. In the spring, stimulate with higher temperature (about 25° C or 77° F). During the growing and blooming seasons, the Gesneria, like all its relatives, must be fed with lime-free fertilizer; the earth must also be free of lime. Under normal conditions, the Gesneria blooms throughout the summer.

Gesneria

POPULAR NAME: **Italian Bellflower**
SCIENTIFIC NAME: *Campanula isophylla*
FAMILY: *Campanulaceae* (Bellflower)

This pretty Bellflower hails from the Ligurian Alps of northern Italy. The original variety possesses light blue blossoms, but there is also a white form, "Alba." Very similar to it is the light blue, Southern Italian Bellflower, *Campanula fragilis* (Star of Bethlehem).

CARE: Both species need lime and are similar in other requirements. They like a location that is bright to semi-shaded, cool and airy. They ought not to be watered too heavily, and application of fertilizer is required only at long intervals. Watering must be reduced in winter and the plants kept in a cool place (3 to 8° C or 37 to 46° F). Both species are very attractive in spring and summer, with a luxuriant growth of blossoms. *Campanula fragilis* blooms a few weeks earlier than the species illustrated here.

Italian Bellflower

POPULAR NAME: **Maurandia**
SCIENTIFIC NAME: *Maurandia barclaiana*
FAMILY: *Scrophulariaceae* (Figwort)

Mexico is the homeland of the Maurandia. From
the purple-blossomed, wild species, cultivated
varieties have been bred, which bloom white,
lilac or pink. Their blooming period extends from
summer to autumn.

CARE: The Maurandia is a popular climbing plant
that prefers an airy location. In summer, it thrives
well in a protected place in the open. Although
usually treated as an annual plant, it is actually a
perennial and can be wintered over at a temperature of 6 to 8° C or 43 to 46° F. It requires
only moderate watering and fertilizing during its
growing period.

Maurandia

POPULAR NAMES: **Slipperwort, Calceolaria**
SCIENTIFIC NAME: *Calceolaria x herbeohybrida*
FAMILY: *Scrophulariaceae* (Figwort)

The plants of the genus Calceolaria inhabit Mexico, and Central and South America. From cross-breeding various wild species, numerous cultivated forms have come into existence, which are known under the collective name of *Calceolaria herbeohybrida*. In addition to varieties patterned in yellow and yellow-brown, there are hybrids that have red, violet, orange and purple blossoms.

CARE: The Slipperwort should be kept in a bright, airy place; however, direct sun is harmful to it. The *herbeohybrida* forms are annuals and can be propagated from seed. Young plants so raised can be wintered over at from 8 to 10° C or 46 to 50° F. The blooming season of the Slipperwort lies between late winter and late spring. The plant needs lots of water and fertilizer and under no circumstances should be allowed to dry out.

Slipperwort

POPULAR NAMES: **Velvet Plant, Purple Passion, Gynura**
SCIENTIFIC NAME: *Gynura aurantiaca*
FAMILY: *Compositae* (Composite)

The Gynura captivates the eye with its velvetlike, hairy, glistening violet leaves. The plant grows to a length of 50 to 100 centimetres (20 to 40 inches) and hails from the mountain forests of Java. The yellow, synantherous (composite) blossoms appear in late summer and autumn.

CARE: Keep the Gynura warm in summer—if possible, in the open—but not in the direct rays of the sun. In winter, a temperature of 14 to 18° C or 57 to 64° F is sufficient, and a brightly lighted location is required. While the Velvet Plant requires a great deal of water in summer, it can be watered less in its resting period. The Gynura does very well as a hanging plant. The young plants especially have a most beautiful appearance. New plants can be propagated from cuttings.

Velvet Plant

POPULAR NAME: **Chlorophytum**
SCIENTIFIC NAME: *Chlorophytum comosum*
FAMILY: *Liliaceae* (Lily)

The green-leaved wild species of the South African Chlorophytum is hardly being cultivated at all today. It has been superseded by the cultured variety "Variegatum," with white-striped leaves. This robust hanging plant sends out runners, on which sprout little offshoot plants, by means of which the Chlorophytum can be effortlessly propagated, since they take root easily. The ornamental white blossoms appear in every season, but the leaves alone are enough to give the plant a striking appearance.

CARE: The Chlorophytum thrives in cold as well as warm rooms, as long as there is plenty of air and indirect light—avoid direct sunlight. The water requirement is governed by the room temperature —the hotter the room is, the more the plant needs to be watered. The Chlorophytum can be wintered over either warm or cold (5 to 7° C or 41 to 45° F).

Chlorophytum

POPULAR NAMES: **African Lily, Lily-of-the-Nile**
SCIENTIFIC NAME: *Agapanthus africanus*
FAMILY: *Liliaceae* (Lily)

The African Lily is a stately tub plant from the
Cape country of South Africa. There are cultivated varieties with white, blue and violet
blossoms, which are derived from crossing *Agapanthus africanus* and *Agapanthus orientalis*, also from
South Africa.

CARE: In summer, choose a warm, sunny place
indoors or out for the African Lily—no blossoms
will develop in the shade. The blooming season
extends through the summer. Water and fertilize
abundantly in summer, but for the winter store
the plant in a bright, airy, but cool place (2 to 8° C
or 36 to 46° F) and water very sparingly.

African Lily

POPULAR NAMES: **Bowstring Hemp, Snake Plant, Sansevieria**
SCIENTIFIC NAME: *Sansevieria trifasciata*
FAMILY: *Liliaceae* (Lily)

The East African Bowstring Hemp and its cultivated varieties are robust plants which are very popular as house plants because of their ornamental leaves. The blooming season is in the spring, but the fragrant blossoms seldom appear on the house plant.

CARE: The warmth-loving Bowstring Hemp should be kept in a sunny or lightly shaded place. In no event should it be kept too wet. Dry summer air suits it quite well. The Bowstring Hemp can winter over at a cool temperature, but never colder than 12° C or 54° F. When in a cool place, it should be watered less frequently than in a warm one. As a potted plant, the Sansevieria may grow over 1 metre (3 feet) high.

Bowstring Hemp

POPULAR NAME: **Aloe**
SCIENTIFIC NAME: *Aloe hybrida*
FAMILY: *Liliaceae* (Lily)

Though the common name of the Aloe is pronounced with only two syllables (Al-o), the Latin name of the genus has three (Al-o-ee). The house plant Aloes hail from South Africa. From the many wild species found there, an array of cultivated forms like the illustrated variety, *strausii*, have been derived. Depending on the species, they bloom in winter, spring or summer. Even without blossoms, most Aloes look very ornamental because of their beautiful leaf patterns. Species that remain small are particularly popular, such as *Aloe aristata, Aloe variegata* and others. Many species are more easily distinguished by their leaves than by their blossoms.

CARE: In summer, give them a bright, sunny place. While they withstand dry household air quite well, they have a normal need for water in the growing season. In the winter resting period, they should be watered very little. The most suitable wintering-over temperature is between 8 and 12° C or 46 to 54° F.

Aloe

POPULAR NAMES: **Clivia, Kafir Lily**
SCIENTIFIC NAME: *Clivia miniata*
FAMILY: *Amaryllidaceae* (Amaryllis)

South Africa is the Clivia's land of origin. The blossoms appear as a rule in spring, but even without them the Clivia is a very ornamental plant. The wild species is hardly grown any longer. In its place are the commoner but more beautiful cultivated varieties. The cultivated variety, "Striata," is especially appealing because of its white or yellowish striped leaves.

CARE: Give the Clivia a warm, bright to semi-shady place in summer, where it can be protected from the direct sun. Water abundantly and sprinkle or spray the plant with water on hot days. From early autumn to mid-winter and after blooming, allow it a resting period in a bright, cool place (8 to 12° C or 46 to 54° F), during which time it should be watered very little. This treatment should induce the plant to bloom again in spring.

Clivia

POPULAR NAMES: **Blood Lily, Red Cape Tulip**
SCIENTIFIC NAME: *Haemanthus coccineus*
FAMILY: *Amaryllidaceae* (Amaryllis)

Just as popular as the red-blooming species illustrated is the white Blood Lily, *Haemanthus albiflos*. Both hail from South Africa and require the same type of care, with one important difference.

CARE: *Haemanthus coccineus* should be kept in a warm, bright place in summer, but protected from the direct rays of the midday sun; however, *Haemanthus albiflos* can withstand the full glare of the sun. The blooming season of both species occurs in spring and early summer. They should be watered regularly during the growing season, but only slightly during its resting season, from mid-autumn to mid-winter. The resting temperature should be no higher than 10 to 12° C or 50 to 54° F.

Blood Lily

POPULAR NAMES: **Amaryllis, Hippeastrum**
SCIENTIFIC NAME: *Hippeastrum hybridum*
FAMILY: *Amaryllidaceae* (Amaryllis)

The *Hippeastrum* hybrids, popularly called "Amaryllis," are the result of numerous crossings, especially of the species *Hippeastrum vittatum* and *Hippeastrum reginae*. Amaryllises are usually purchased in the form of a bulb, because it is fascinating to watch the tall flower stalk shoot up from the soil, soon followed by the opening of the handsome blossoms. Depending on the variety, the flowers may be red, pink or white. The sword-shaped leaves appear either before the blossoms or along with them. Amaryllises reach the peak of their blooming season between early winter and the middle of spring.

CARE: During the growing period, which lasts until late summer, *Hippeastrum hybridum* should be kept in a bright, warm place, but protected from the glare of the sun. Water abundantly and fertilize every 10 days. In the autumn, the part of the Amaryllis above ground withers away and the bulb rests from then until winter begins. Do not water at all during this time, and keep the bulb cool (12° C or 54° F) and practically dried out. When the new growth starts up and the plant has reached a height of about 10 centimetres (4 inches), put the plant in a warmer place (20 to 25° C or 68 to 77° F). At the same time, start

Amaryllis

watering again and gradually increase the amount of water each time.

POPULAR NAME: **Stripe-Leaf Amaryllis**
SCIENTIFIC NAME: *Hippeastrum reticulatum*
FAMILY: *Amaryllidaceae* (Amaryllis)

The blossoms of this rare Amaryllis from southern Brazil and its cultured variety, "Striatifolium," appear in the autumn season and give off a pleasant fragrance.

CARE: In summer, keep it moist and warm; in winter, cool and dry.

NOTE: The true Amaryllis consists of a single species, *Amaryllis belladonna,* the belladonna lily of South Africa. The *Hippeastrum* genus is closely related.

Stripe-Leaf Amaryllis

POPULAR NAMES: **Nidularium, Blushing Cup**
SCIENTIFIC NAME: *Nidularium fulgens*
FAMILY: *Bromeliaceae* (Pineapple)

Members of the genus *Nidularium* (so called because the shape and arrangement of the flower heads give the appearance of a nest, *nidus* in Latin) are epiphytic Bromeliads. *Nidularium fulgens* hails from southern Brazil. The blue blossoms (not open in the illustration) appear throughout the summer, growing out of the bright scarlet inflorescence.
CARE: In summer, the Nidularium requires a warm (20° C or 68° F), airy place in shade and must be watered abundantly. In winter, it gets by with less water and a temperature of 15 to 18° C or 59 to 64° F.

CARE OF BROMELIADS

The pineapple plants, or Bromeliads, are natives of tropical America. A great many of them live like many orchids, epiphytically on trees or rocks. While epiphytic orchids absorb a great deal of their nourishment through their aerial roots and store it in their so-called pseudo-bulbs, many Bromeliads collect it in the funnels formed by their leaf rosettes. For this reason, Bromeliads should be watered—always with rain water—directly into this funnel, from which the blossoms will grow forth later. The funnel should always be kept full

Nidularium

of water, and in addition, during the growing period, the plant itself should be watered in accordance with its needs. The difficulties experienced in watering orchids do not exist with the pineapple family. But they do have the same requirements in respect to humidity. Their blossoms are not outstanding, but the lively coloration of the involucre (topmost whorl of leaves supporting the blossoms) which surrounds the blossoms, are often of great beauty and intensity of coloration. The involucres outlast the actual blossom by a long time. After blossoming, the plant dies, but in the meantime, offshoot plants—so-called "children"—have developed. These provide for steady renewal of the plant. To the great number of beautiful wild species have been added many cultivated varieties, which are often even more ornamental.

POPULAR NAME: **Striped Torch**
SCIENTIFIC NAME: *Guzmania monostachya (Guzmania tricolor)*
FAMILY: *Bromeliaceae* (Pineapple)

The Guzmanias are warmth-loving, like all other genera of this family. The Striped Torch, one of the finest and most beautiful, comes from the West Indies and from Central and South America. The white blossoms appear in summer; the beautiful inflorescence with red bracts, changing to green and brown stripes, however, is unfortunately of short duration.

Striped Torch

CARE: *Guzmania* should be cared for the same as *Nidularium* species, but in a somewhat warmer location.

POPULAR NAMES: **Blue Tillandsia, Blue-Flowered Torch**
SCIENTIFIC NAME: *Tillandsia lindeniana (Tillandsia lindenii, Tillandsia cyanea)*
FAMILY: *Bromeliaceae* (Pineapple)

This splendid plant is an epiphytic Bromeliad without funnels, originally from Ecuador. The blue blossoms unfold in late autumn and winter; the pink bracts last a long time. The care of these warmth- and shade-loving plants is like that of *Nidularium fulgens*.

Blue Tillandsia

POPULAR NAME: **Scarlet Star**
SCIENTIFIC NAME: *Guzmania lingulata (Caraguata splendens)*
FAMILY: *Bromeliaceae* (Pineapple)

South America and the Antilles are the homeland of this stately, epiphytic Bromeliad. A spray of brilliant scarlet bracts surrounds the cluster of white flowers. The well known hybrid *Gusmania x intermedia* is partly derived from one of the subspecies of *Guzmania lingulata*.

CARE: *Guzmania lingulata* is cared for the same as *Nidularium fulgens,* but should be kept in a warmer place. The blooming season is not definite, being influenced by growing conditions.

Scarlet Star

POPULAR NAMES: **Billbergia, Queen's Tears**
SCIENTIFIC NAME: *Billbergia nutans*
FAMILY: *Bromeliaceae* (Pineapple)

Billbergia nutans, along with its hybrid varieties, is among the finest Bromeliads for pot culture. It originated in Brazil, Argentina, and Paraguay, and withstands dry air better than most of the species discussed here. The hanging blue-green blossoms appear in winter, contrasting beautifully with the red of the involucre, but unfortunately the inflorescence does not last very long.

CARE: *Billbergia nutans* must be kept in a place that is sunny to semi-shaded and cooler (15 to 18° C or 59 to 64° F) than for other Bromeliads. In summer and during the blooming season, water plentifully. Propagation of this especially sturdy species by means of layering offers no difficulties. In layering, a branch or shoot is bent down and covered with soil, to allow it to root. In *air-layering*, a branch is partially severed and wrapped in a rooting material at the point of fracture.

Billbergia

POPULAR NAMES: **Vriesia, Lobster Claws**
SCIENTIFIC NAME: *Vriesia carinata (Vriesia psittacina)*
FAMILY: *Bromeliaceae* (Pineapple)

The Vriesia, a very variable species, hails from Brazil. It grows small and for that reason is well suited for a house plant. A number of cultivated varieties have been bred from the wild species. The green, red and yellow bracts of the flower head have a striking appearance when they appear in autumn and winter. The blossoms themselves are yellow (they have not yet opened on the specimen in the photo).

CARE: *Vriesia carinata* should be kept in a shady place and rather warm (18 to 22° C or 64 to 72° F). During the resting period, which comes immediately after blooming, the temperature should be kept at about 18° C or 64° F. Put the plant aside in a bright place and water sparingly.

Vriesia

POPULAR NAME: **Aechmea**
SCIENTIFIC NAME: *Aechmea fasciata*
FAMILY: *Bromeliaceae* (Pineapple)

This well liked Bromeliad originated in Brazil. It
stands out just as much as *Billbergia nutans,* and is
even more attractive. The blossoms, which appear
in summer, are first blue, then turn red later on in
the blooming season. The beautiful inflorescence
outlasts the blossoms, surviving far into the winter.
CARE: *Aechmea fasciata* withstands dry household
air quite well, contrary to most other Bromeliads.
It requires a semi-shady, not excessively warm
location, and is cared for like the other members
of the pineapple family described here.

Aechmea

POPULAR NAME: **Vriesia, Flaming Sword**
SCIENTIFIC NAME: *Vriesia splendens (V. speciosa)*
FAMILY: *Bromeliaceae* (Pineapple)

Along with the wild species, which comes from the Guianas, and its variety *major,* there are several especially fine hybrids on the market, mostly crossbreeds of various subspecies. The name "Flaming Sword" is given to these cross-breeds as a group. *Vriesia splendens* loves warmth, and it should be kept in a place that is shady but not too dark.
CARE: Its care and propagation are the same as for other Bromeliads. The blooming season of the original Flaming Sword variety occurs in winter, but the hybrids also bloom at other times of the year. The lovely yellow single blossoms—not seen in the photograph—grow out of the bright red floral axis. Even without its flower heads, *Vriesia splendens* presents a very striking appearance, due to its banded leaves.

Vriesia

SCIENTIFIC NAME: *Calathea makoyana (Maranta makoyana)*
FAMILY: *Marantaceae* (Maranta)

Calatheas inhabit the warm, moist forests of Brazil. Their blossoms are rather plain-looking and appear but seldom in potted plants. The beautiful leaves are what make these plants desirable. The underside of the leaves shows the same pattern as the upper side, but in red instead of green.

CARE: In their homeland, Calatheas are always accustomed to high humidity, and therefore are quite sensitive to dry household air. Proper humidity can be best achieved by placing Calatheas in close association with other plants and by sprinkling with soft water. Full sun harms Calatheas, so keep them in a warm, shaded to semi-shaded place and water them plentifully. During the growing season, the temperature should hover around 18 to 22° C or 64 to 72° F; in winter, it must not drop below 16° C or 61° F.

Calathea

POPULAR NAMES: **Calathea, Rattlesnake Plant**
SCIENTIFIC NAME: *Calathea insignis*
FAMILY: *Marantaceae* (Maranta)

Like *Calathea makoyana, Calathea insignis* is a native of the tropical forests of Brazil. The wild species grows up to 2 metres (6½ feet) high, but is not often sold as a house plant; however, a very similar cultivated variety is available. In the wild species, the underside of the leaf is green; in the cultivated variety, it is patterned with red.

CARE: Both plants of the Maranta family described here require the same kind of care. Species of the closely related *Maranta* genus, which also originate in Brazil, should be treated the same as Calathea.

Calathea

POPULAR NAMES: **Canary Island Date Palm, Feather Palm**

SCIENTIFIC NAME: *Phoenix canariensis*

FAMILY: *Palmaceae* (Palm)

This Feather Palm from the Canary Islands is only one of the many date palms that can be cultivated as a house plant, but it is one of the hardiest. It does not grow as large as the true date palm, *Phoenix dactylifera,* which can be raised from the seed of the edible fruit.

CARE: In summer, the Feather Palm should be kept in an airy place outdoors, in full sunlight. At this time, water abundantly and wash accumulated dust from the leaves regularly. In the resting period, from about mid-autumn until mid-winter, water sparingly. While most palms require a lowest temperature range of 10 to 15° C or 50 to 59° F in winter, *Phoenix canariensis* can get by at a temperature just slightly above freezing point (0° C or 32° F).

Canary Island Date Palm

POPULAR NAMES: **Wandering Jew, Zebrina**
SCIENTIFIC NAME: *Zebrina pendula (Tradescantia zebrina)*
FAMILY: *Commelinaceae* (Spiderwort)

The Zebrina is a fine, trailing perennial from Mexico. It gets its Latin generic name from the striping of its leaves, which resembles that of a zebra. The blooming season occurs in the late spring and early summer, but the small, pink blossoms seldom appear in house plant culture.

CARE: The Wandering Jew is a hanging plant which must be given a bright to semi-shaded location. Water it plentifully during the summer growing season—the earth-ball in the pot should be kept constantly moist. Water it less in winter. During its resting period, it can be left in a heated room, or it can winter over in a cooler place, however not under 12 to 14° C or 54 to 57° F, if watering is reduced accordingly.

Wandering Jew

POPULAR NAMES: **Ivy Arum, Scindapsus, Pothos**
SCIENTIFIC NAME: *Scindapsus aureus*
FAMILY: *Araceae* (Arum)

This climbing plant, which is rather variable in its leaf coloration, hails from the Solomon Islands of the South Pacific. It is commonly called "Pothos" by florists, although that is properly the generic name of a related plant. It does not bloom when cultivated as a house plant.

CARE: It should be kept in a place that is bright to semi-shaded and always moist. Normal summer temperatures are high enough for it; during its winter resting period it should not be allowed to get colder than 12 to 14° C or 54 to 57° F. During the growing season fertilize it once a week. A related species, *Scindapsus pictus,* with blue or whitish-blue dots on its leaves, requires somewhat more warmth (at least 18° C or 64° F) and higher humidity; otherwise it is treated the same. The popular, green-leaved Climbing Philodendron, *Philodendron scandens*, resembles *Scindapsus aureus* and is cared for in the same way.

Ivy Arum

POPULAR NAME: **Spathiphyllum**
SCIENTIFIC NAME: *Spathiphyllum wallisii*
FAMILY: *Araceae* (Arum)

This Spathiphyllum hails from Colombia and blooms from spring to autumn. Plants of the Arum family have a distinctive inflorescence consisting of a spathe, or large bract, enclosing a spadix, or spike of small flowers. The spathe is often bright red, yellow, white or other hues. In this species it is white. Even without blossoms, the plant looks very attractive because of its beautiful dark green leaves.

CARE: Spathiphyllum needs a warm, shady spot with rather high humidity, but it will temporarily withstand lower temperatures so long as they do not drop below 14 to 16° C or 57 to 61° F. Spray the plant frequently with water, but avoid wetting the spathe. During the summer growing season, water abundantly; in winter, moderately. The lowest temperature noted above should also be maintained during the winter.

Spathiphyllum

POPULAR NAMES: **Split-Leaf Philodendron, Ceriman**
SCIENTIFIC NAME: *Monstera deliciosa (Philodendron pertusum)*
FAMILY: *Araceae* (Arum)

This Mexican climber is one of the best-liked and finest green-leaved plants for pot culture. It is a foliage plant—blossoms develop rarely when it is grown as a house plant. Especially popular is the small-leaved variety *borsigiana*.

CARE: The Split-Leaf Philodendron should be placed in a bright to semi-shaded and rather warm location. The leaves will not split unless the plant is exposed to direct daylight (not sunlight). In winter, the temperature should not be allowed to drop below 12 to 18° C or 54 to 64° F. Water plentifully in summer, but reduce watering during the winter resting period. During its growing season, fertilize the plant regularly. Either spray the leaves or wash them off frequently. Do not cut or damage the aerial roots, as these are necessary to the life of the plant. It is best to let them strike root in the pot.

Split-Leaf Philodendron

POPULAR NAMES: **Dieffenbachia, Dumb Cane**
SCIENTIFIC NAME: *Dieffenbachia x bausei*
FAMILY: *Araceae* (Arum)

Many green or variegated wild species of Dieffenbachia are to be found along with numerous
horticultural cross-breeds of this beautiful leaf
plant. *Dieffenbachia x bausei* is the product of a
cross between two Brazilian wild species, *Dieffenbachia picta* and *Dieffenbachia weiri*. The inconspicuous blossoms seldom develop in pot culture—
the handsome leaves are the principal attraction.
CARE: To thrive well, the Dieffenbachia requires a
semi-shaded, warm location with high humidity.
Water it plentifully in summer, but less in winter,
its resting period. At this time, too, the temperature should not drop below 14 to 16° C or 57 to
61° F. *The sap of the Dieffenbachia is poisonous to the
taste.*

Dieffenbachia

POPULAR NAMES: **Flamingo Flower, Flame Plant**
SCIENTIFIC NAME: *Anthurium scherzerianum*
FAMILY: *Araceae* (Arum)

Wild species from tropical Costa Rica and Guatemala are the ancestors of many varieties and cross-breeds, many with a red spathe, many with white, yellowish, and speckled coloration.

CARE: The Flamingo Flower requires a lot of humidity and warmth, but must be protected from the direct rays of the sun. Sprinkle it frequently with soft water. In winter, it should be kept rather warm (around 16 to 20° C or 61 to 68° F). During its resting period, from late autumn to early winter, water sparingly. Water it heavily in the growing period. The Flamingo Flower has no decided blooming season; however, it blooms most often in the spring.

Flamingo Flower

POPULAR NAMES: **Andraea's Flamingo Flower,
Andraea's Anthurium, Oilcloth Flower, Fall Flower**
SCIENTIFIC NAME: *Anthurium andraenum*
FAMILY: *Araceae* (Arum)

The wild species of this Colombian plant is no
longer cultivated. Under the designation *Anthurium
x cultorum* is found an abundance of horticultural
varieties derived from *Anthurium andraeanum*. *Anthurium andraeanum* is larger than *scherzerianum* and
has an erect, not curved, spadix. It blooms the
year round.

CARE: These plants require constant moisture,
but also must have good drainage, so that water
does not stand about the roots. They require a
somewhat higher temperature than *scherzerianum*.
They can use morning sun but not much direct
sunlight.

Andraea's Flamingo Flower

POPULAR NAMES: **Calla Lily** (U.S.), **Arum-Lily** (U.K.)
SCIENTIFIC NAME: *Zantedeschia aethiopica*
FAMILY: *Araceae* (Arum)

The wild species, which inhabits swampy, but dry in summer, meadows of the Cape region of South Africa has given rise to a number of cultivated forms. The large white petal-like spathe encloses a brilliant yellow spadix.
CARE: The Calla Lily likes a warm, not too sunny, location in the growing season, with a relatively high humidity. It blooms from mid-winter to early spring; however, the blooming season can be postponed by planting the rhizome later than usual. After blooming, it requires a resting period from late spring into summer, in a warm, sunny place and should not be watered. At this time, the foliage will dry off. In mid-summer, begin to water it again. In its growing season, the Calla Lily requires heavy fertilization and a great deal of water—in fact it even tolerates water standing in the pot. During the winter, a temperature of 8 to 10° C or 46 to 50° F is enough. In mid-winter, the temperature should be gradually increased.

Calla Lily

SCIENTIFIC NAME: *Caladium x hortulanum*
FAMILY: *Araceae* (Arum)

Caladium x hortulanum is the designation for the many cultivated varieties resulting from the crossbreeding of various South American species. Their beautiful leaves come in many combinations of red, white, green and cream, in a wide range of patterns. The not very striking blossoms appear in the spring.

CARE: Caladiums should have a location that is warm and semi-shady, with high humidity. They are very sensitive to drafts. During the growing season take care that the temperature remains high (25° C or 77° F) and water and fertilize plentifully. From mid-summer on, reduce watering, and let the plants die down. Keep the tubers warm throughout the winter (20° C or 68° F), but do not let them dry out completely. Plant the tubers again in mid-winter. *Caladiums are poisonous if eaten.*

Caladium

POPULAR NAME: **Cattleya**
SCIENTIFIC NAME: *Cattleya maxima,* var. *marchettiana*
FAMILY: *Orchidaceae* (Orchid)

Cattleya maxima hails from South America, and blooms in autumn or winter. Orchid keeping requires some experience and it is better to try your hand at growing *Cattleya maxima* after you had some success with Cattleyas that are easier to grow. *Cattleya bowringiana* and *Cattleya skinneri,* for example, are easy to care for as house plants. All Cattleyas pass through a restricted resting period in which the root-ball must be kept practically dry. During the growing season, they should be kept warm and in high humidity, in a shady place.

ORCHID CARE

Orchids require careful attention and their demands vary from species to species. With many species, the resting period must be severely restricted, otherwise they will not blossom. Every mood of the plant must be closely watched. When the tips of the new growth appear, end the resting period gradually. Since epiphytic orchids obtain a great deal of their nourishment and moisture from the air, high humidity (at least 60 per cent) and good ventilation are necessary to the life of the plant. Dampness can be achieved by sprinkling

Cattleya

or spraying and by placing water-filled dishes under the pots, but the water must not come in contact with the pot. All orchids should be watered carefully with luke-warm rain water.

Species preferring less warmth thrive best as house plants, since it is easier to provide them with a relatively high humidity. All orchids should be set in special, water-permeable vegetal material instead of soil. Ask your florist about this.

POPULAR NAME: **Skinner's Lycaste**
SCIENTIFIC NAME: *Lycaste skinneri*
FAMILY: *Orchidaceae* (Orchid)

This delicate pink orchid is along with the yellow-blooming species *Lycaste aromatica* and *Lycaste cruenta,* recommended for the beginner. *Lycaste skinneri* is noted for its very large blossoms, whose blooming season extends through most of the autumn season. The Lycastes need a great deal of water during the growing season and are among those few orchids which must be fertilized. They prefer a bright, temperate location, without glaring sun. In their resting period from autumn until winter, hardly water them at all. *Lycaste skinneri* drops its leaves after blooming.

Skinner's Lycaste

POPULAR NAME: **Lady Slipper**
SCIENTIFIC NAME: *Paphiopedilum venustum* (incorrectly called *Cypripedium*)
FAMILY: *Orchidaceae* (Orchid)

This orchid from the region of the Himalayas is not epiphytic—it grows in soil. It should be kept at moderate temperature (14 to 18° C or 57 to 64° F) in a shady place. It blooms in winter. The Paphiopedilums do not undergo any kind of restrictive resting period, except that following the blooming season they should be kept somewhat dryer for a few weeks. Excessive water allowed to stand above ground-level in the pot will damage the plant, as it does all orchids. Other fine species of the genus are *Paphiopedilum fairieanum*, *P. sukhakulii*, *P. callosum* (all of which require higher temperatures than *venustum*).

Lady Slipper

POPULAR NAME: **Bird's-Bill Oncidium**
SCIENTIFIC NAME: *Oncidium ornithorhynchum*
FAMILY: *Orchidaceae* (Orchid)

The Bird's-Bill Oncidium is an epiphytic orchid from Guatemala and Mexico that is suitable for the beginner. It blooms in autumn and winter, and should be kept bright and cool (about 8 to 12° C or 46 to 54° F), but out of the direct sun. The mid-day temperature may be higher. Water it frequently during the growing season, but in the resting period after blooming, water only a little. Many other Oncidiums, such as the yellow-blooming *Oncidium varicosum*, are more difficult to care for than this species.

Bird's-Bill Oncidium

POPULAR NAMES: **Odontoglossum, Tiger Orchid**
SCIENTIFIC NAME: *Odontoglossum grande*
FAMILY: *Orchidaceae* (Orchid)

This handsome, large-blossomed epiphytic orchid from Mexico and Guatemala is often recommended for beginners, in spite of the fact that it often fails to bloom. Its blooming season takes place in autumn and winter, during its resting period. When the floral spikes are sufficiently developed, water the plant even though it is in its resting period, until blooming is over. Other species of the genus are more dependable, especially the white, fragrant *Odontoglossum pulchellum*, the brownish-pink *Odontoglossum bictoniense* and the white-brown *Odontoglossum rosii*.

CARE: Odontoglossums should not be kept in a highly heated room. In summer, they can be kept in a shady place outdoors, but should be sprayed. Water plentifully in summer, but very little in the winter resting period. With *Odontoglossum grande,* spray only the outside of the pot.

Odontoglossum

POPULAR NAME: **Bifrenaria**
SCIENTIFIC NAME: *Bifrenaria harrisoniae*
FAMILY: *Orchidaceae* (Orchid)

Bifrenaria harrisoniae, a native of Brazil, is one of the
most undemanding of orchids and for this reason
is especially suitable for the beginner. The blossoms
of this stately epiphyte open in the spring and are
long-lasting. After blooming, allow the plant a
short resting period of about 4 weeks. Like all
orchids, the Bifrenaria needs high humidity, and
should be kept in a cool, bright and airy location.
But, be careful with watering—luke-warm rain
water is ideal. Do not let the roots stand in water.
During the winter resting period, the night-time
temperature may drop as low as 14° C or 57° F.

Bifrenaria

The Dendrobiums, scattered over Asia, Oceania
and Australia number well over 1,000 species,
many with differing requirements. The popular
Dendrobium nobile and its many hybrids should be
kept in a place that is temperate to cool. *Dendrobium thyrsiflorum* from Burma (illustrated) prefers
more warmth—it should be kept in a warm, bright
place in summer; it needs a fair amount of water
then. In winter, keep it cooler (around 18° C or
64° F) and give it hardly any water. The blooming
season lasts from late winter to mid-spring, but
the beautiful blossoms last only a few days. The
yellow-blossomed species, *Dendrobium densiflorum*
and *Dendrobium fimbriatum,* have an inflorescence
similar to *thyrsiflorum* and require the same care.

Dendrobium

POPULAR NAME: **Crested Coelogyne**
SCIENTIFIC NAME: *Coelogyne cristata*
FAMILY: *Orchidaceae* (Orchid)

The Coelogyne is an epiphytic orchid from the temperate altitudes of the Himalaya region. During the growing season in summer, it should be kept in a temperate place (14 to 18° C or 57 to 64° F), quite airy and bright. The blooming season begins with winter (Christmas), and extends into the middle of spring. The blossoms should not be sprayed. During the short resting period after blooming, reduce watering sharply. The *pseudo-bulbs*—actually, thickened parts of the stalk—should not be allowed to shrivel too much. Take care in summer that the orchid does not get too warm. Many other species of the genus *Coelogyne* hail from tropical Asia and are, unlike the *Coelogyne cristata*, treated like hot-house orchids.

Crested Coelogyne

SCIENTIFIC NAME INDEX

GENERAL INDEX